Charles H. Ross

The Book of Cats

A Chit-chat Chronicle of Feline Facts and Fancies, Legendary, Lyrica

Charles H. Ross

The Book of Cats
A Chit-chat Chronicle of Feline Facts and Fancies, Legendary, Lyrica

ISBN/EAN: 9783744792387

Printed in Europe, USA, Canada, Australia, Japan

Cover: Foto ©Andreas Hilbeck / pixelio.de

More available books at **www.hansebooks.com**

THE
BOOK OF CATS.

A Chit-Chat Chronicle

OF

FELINE FACTS AND FANCIES, LEGENDARY, LYRICAL

MEDICAL, MIRTHFUL AND MISCELLANEOUS.

BY CHARLES H. ROSS.

WITH

Twenty Illustrations by the Author.

LONDON:

GRIFFITH AND FARRAN,

(SUCCESSORS TO NEWBERY AND HARRIS),

CORNER OF ST. PAUL'S CHURCHYARD.

MDCCCLXVIII.

LONDON :

WERTHEIMER, LEA AND CO., PRINTERS, CIRCUS PLACE,
FINSBURY CIRCUS.

NOTICE.

—0—

THE Author would thankfully receive any well-authenticated anecdotes respecting Cats, with the view of incorporating them with the work, in the event of a fresh Edition being called for.

SPRING COTTAGE, FULHAM.
November, 1867.

CONTENTS.

—o—

CHAPTER I.

THE BOOK OF CATS.

CHAPTER I.

B

CHAPTER I.

—o—

Of the reason why this Book was written, and of several sorts of Cats which are not strictly Zoological.

—o—

ONE day, ever so long ago, it struck me that I should like to try and write a book about Cats. I mentioned the idea to some of my friends : the first burst out laughing at the end of my opening sentence, so I refrained from entering into further details. The second said there were a hundred books about Cats already. The third said, " Nobody would

read it," and added, "Besides, what do you know
of the subject?" and before I had time to begin to
tell him, said he expected it was very little. "Why
not Dogs?" asked one friend of mine, hitting upon
the notion as though by inspiration. "Or Horses,"
said some one else ; "or Pigs ; or, look here, this is
the finest notion of all :—

'THE BOOK OF DONKIES,

'BY ONE OF THE FAMILY !'"

Somewhat disheartened by the reception my
little project had met with, I gave up the idea for
awhile, and went to work upon other things. I
cannot exactly remember what I did, or how much,
but my book about Cats was postponed *sine die*,
and in the meantime I made some inquiries.

I searched high and low; I consulted Lady Cust's
little volume; I bought Mr. Beeton's book; I read
up Buffon and Bell, and Frank Buckland; I eagerly
perused the amusing pages of the Rev. Mr. Wood;
I looked through two or three hundred works of
one sort and another, and as many old newspapers
and odd numbers of defunct periodicals, and
although I daresay I have overlooked some of
the very best, I have really taken a great deal of

trouble, and sincerely hope that I shall be able to amuse you by my version of what other people have had to tell, with a good many things which have not yet appeared in print, that I have to tell myself.

One thing I found out very early in my researches, and that was, that nine out of ten among my authorities were prejudiced against the animal about which they wrote, and furthermore, that they knew very little indeed upon the subject. Take for instance our old friend Mavor, who thus mis-teaches the young idea in his celebrated Spelling Book. "Cats," says Mr. Mavor, "have less sense than dogs, and their attachment is chiefly to the house ; but the dog's is to the persons who inhabit it." Need I tell the reader who has thought it worth his while to learn anything of the Cat's nature, that Mr. Mavor's was a vulgar and erroneous belief, and that there are countless instances on record where Cats have shown the most devoted and enduring attachment to those who have kindly treated them. Again, nothing can be more unjust than to call Cats cruel. If such a word as cruel could be applied to a creature without reason, few animals could be found more cruel than a Robin Redbreast, which we have all determined to make a pet of since somebody wrote that pretty fable about the "Babes in the Wood." And apropos of the Robin, do you remember Canning's verses?

> "Tell me, tell me, gentle Robin,
> What is it sets thy heart a-throbbing?
> Is it that Grimalkin fell
> Hath killed thy father or thy mother,
> Thy sister or thy brother,
> Or any other?
> Tell me but that,
> And I'll kill the Cat.
>
> But stay, little Robin, did you ever spare,
> A grub on the ground or a fly in the air?
> No, that you never did, I'll swear;
> So I won't kill the Cat,
> That's flat."

But all the cruel and unjust things that have been said about poor pussy I will tell you in another chapter. I mean to try and begin at the beginning. In the first place, what is the meaning of the word "Cat." Let us look in the dictionary. A Cat, according to Dr. Johnson, is "a domestick animal that catches mice." But the word has one or two other meanings, for instance:—

In thieves' slang the word "Cat" signifies a lady's muff, and "to free a cat" to steal a muff. Among soldiers and sailors a "Cat" means something very unpleasant indeed, with nine tingling lashes or tails, so called, from the scratches they leave on the skin, like the claws of a cat.

A Cat is also the name for a tackle or combination of pulleys, to suspend the anchor at the cat's-head of a ship.

Cat-harping is the name for a purchase of ropes employed to brace in the shrouds of the lower masts behind their yards.

The Cat-fall is the name of a rope employed upon the Cat-head. Two little holes astern, above the Gun-room ports, are called Cat-holes.

A Cat's-paw is a particular turn in the bight of a rope made to hook a tackle in; and the light air perceived in a calm by a rippling on the surface of the water, is known by the same name.

A kind of double tripod with six feet, intended to hold a plate before the fire and so constructed that, in whatever position it is placed, three of the legs rest on the ground, is called a Cat, from the belief that however a Cat may be thrown, she always falls on her feet.

Cat-salt is a name given by our salt-workers to a very beautifully granulated kind of common salt.

Cat's-eye or Sun-stone of the Turks is a kind of gem found chiefly in Siberia. It is very hard and semi-transparent, and has different points from whence the light is reflected with a kind of yellowish radiation somewhat similar to the eyes of cats.

Catkins are imperfect flowers hanging from trees in the manner of a rope or cat's-tail.

Cat's-meat, Cat-thyme, and Cat's-foot are the names of herbs ; Cat's head of an apple, and also of a kind of fossil.   Cat-silver is a fossil.   Cat's-tail is a seed or a long round substance growing on a nut-tree.

A Cat-fish is a shark in the West Indies.   Guanahani, or Cat Island, a small island of the Bahama group, in the West Indies, is supposed to be so called because wild Cats of large size used to infest it, but I can find no particulars upon the subject in the works of writers on the West Indies.

In the North of England, a common expression of contempt is to call a person Cat-faced.   Artists call portraits containing two-thirds of the figure Kit-cat size.   With little boys in the street a Cat is a dreadfully objectionable plaything, roughly cut out of a stick or piece of wood, and sharpened at each end.   Those whose way to business lies through low neighbourhoods, and who venture upon short cuts, well know from bitter experience that at a certain period of the year the tip-cat season sets in with awful severity, and then it is not safe for

TIP-CAT.

Page 8.

such as have eyes to lose, to wander where the epidemic rages.

In the North, however, the same game is called "Piggie." I learn by the newspaper that a young woman at Leeds nearly lost her eye-sight by a blow from one of these piggies or cats, and the magistrates sent the boy who was the cause of it to an industrial school, ordering his father to pay half-a-crown a week for his maintenance.

The shrill whistle indulged in upon the first night of a pantomime by those young gentlemen with the figure six curls in the front row of the gallery are denominated cat-calls. This is, I am given to understand, a difficult art to acquire—I know I have tried very hard myself and can't; and to arrive at perfection you must lose a front tooth. Such a thing has been known before this, as a young costermonger having one of his front teeth pulled out to enable him to whistle well. Let us hope that his talent was properly appreciated in the circles in which he moved.

With respect to cat-calls or cat-cals, also termed cat-pipes, it would appear that there was an instrument by that name used by the audiences at the theatre, the noise of which was very different to that made by whistling through the fingers, as now practised. In the *Covent Garden Journal* for 1810 the O. P. Riots are thus spoken of :—" Mr. Kemble made his appearance in the costume of ' Macbeth,' and, amid vollies of hissing, hooting, groans, and cat-calls, seemed as though he meant to speak a steril and pointless addressa nnounced for the occasion."

In book iii. chap. vi. of *Joseph Andrews*, occurs this passage :—" You would have seen cities in embroidery transplanted from the boxes to the pit, whose ancient inhabitants were exalted to the galleries, where they played upon cat-calls."

In Lloyd's *Law Student* we find :—

> " By law let others strive to gain renown !
> Florio's a gentleman, a man o' th' town.
> He nor courts clients, or the law regarding,
> Hurries from Nando's down to Covent Garden.
> Zethe's a scholar—mark him in the pit,
> With critic Cat-call sound the stops of wit."

In *Chetwood's History of the Stage* (1741), there is a story of a sea-officer who was much plagued by "a couple of sparks, prepared with their offensive instruments, vulgarly termed Cat-calls ;" and describes how "the squeak was stopped in the middle by a blow from the officer, which he gave with so strong a will that his child's trumpet was struck through his cheek."

The Cat-call used at theatres in former times was a small circular whistle, composed of two plates of tin of about the size of a half-penny perforated by a hole in the centre, and connected by a band or border of the same metal about one-eighth of an inch thick. The instrument was readily concealed within the mouth, and the perpetrator of the noise could not be detected.

There used to be a public-house of some notoriety at the corner of Downing-street, next to King-street, called the "*Cat and Bagpipes.*" It was also a chop house used by many persons connected with the public offices in the neighbourhood. George Rose, so well known in after life as the friend of Pitt, Clerk of the Parliament, Secretary of the Treasury, etc., and executor of the Earl of March-mont, but then "a bashful young man," was one of the frequenters of this tavern.

Madame Catalini is thus alluded to with dis-respectful abbreviation of her name in *a new song on Covent Garden Theatre*, printed and sold by J. Pitts, No. 14, Great St. Andrew-street, Seven Dials.

" This noble building, to be sure, has beauty without bounds,
It cost upwards of one hundred and fifty thousand pounds ;
They've Madame Catalini there to open her white throat,
But to hear your foreign singers I would not give a groat ;

So haste away unto the play, whose name has reached the skies,
And when the Cati ope's her mouth, oh how she'll catch the flies !"

It was once upon a time the trick of a country-
man to bring a Cat to market in a bag, and sub-
stitute it for a sucking pig in another bag, which
he sold to the unwary when he got the chance.   If
the trick was discovered prematurely, it was called
letting the cat out of the bag—if not—he that made
the bad bargain was said to have bought a pig in
a poke.   To turn the Cat in the pan, according to
Bacon, is when that which a man says to another
he says it as if another had said it to him.

There is a kind of ship, too, called a Cat, a vessel
formed on the Norwegian model, of about 600 tons
burthen.   That was the sort of cat that brought the
great Dick Whittington, of "turn again" memory,
his fortune.   Do you remember how sorry you
were to find out the truth ?   Do you recollect what
a pang it cost you when first you heard that Robin-
son Crusoe was not true ?   I shall never forget
how vexed and disappointed I was at hearing that
Dick Turpin never did ride to York on his famous
mare Black Bess, and that no such person as
William Tell ever existed, and that that beautiful
story about the apple was only a beautiful story
after all.

CHAPTER II.

—o—

Of some Wicked Stories that have been told about Cats.

—o—

"I DO not love a Cat," says a popular author, often quoted ; " his disposition is mean and suspicious. A friendship of years is cancelled in a moment by an accidental tread on the tail. He spits, twirls his tail of malignity, and shuns you, turning back as he goes off a staring vindictive face full of horrid oaths and unforgiveness, seeming to say, ' Perdition catch you ! I hate you for ever.' But the Dog is my delight. Tread on his tail, he expresses for a moment the uneasiness of his feelings, but in a moment the complaint is ended : he runs round you, jumps up against you, seems to declare his sorrow for complaining, as it was not intentionally done,—nay, to make himself the aggressor, and begs, by whinings and lickings, that the master will think of it no more." No sentiments could be more popular with some gentlemen. In the same way there are those who would like to beat their wives, and for them to come and kiss the hand that struck them in all humility. It is not only when hurt by accident that the dog comes whining round its master. The lashed hound crawls back and licks the boot that kicked him, and so makes friends again. Pussy will not do that though. If you want to be friendly with a cat on Tuesday, you must not kick him on Monday. You must not fondle him one moment and illtreat him the next, or he will be shy of your advances. This really human way of behaving makes Pussy unpopular.

I am afraid that if it were to occur to one of our legislators to tax the Cats, the feline slaughter would be fearful. Every one is fond of dogs, and yet Mr. Edmund Yates, travelling by water to Greenwich last June, said that the journey was pleasingly diversified by practical and nasal demonstrations of the efficient working of the Dog-tax. " No fewer than 292 bodies of departed canines, in various stages of decomposition, were floating off Greenwich during the space of seven days in the previous month, seventy-eight of which were found jammed in the chains and landing-stages of the " Dreadnought " hospital ship, thereby enhancing the salubrity of that celebrated hot-house for sick seamen." And I cannot venture to repeat the incredible stories of the numbers said to have been taken from the Regent's Canal.

There are some persons who profess to have a great repugnance to Cats. King Henry III. of France, a poor, weak, dissipated creature, was one of these. According to Conrad Gesner, men have been known to lose their strength, perspire violently, and even faint at the sight of a cat. Others are said to have gone even further than this, for some have fainted at a cat's picture, or when they have been in a room where such a picture was concealed, or when the picture was as far off as the next room. It was supposed that this sensitiveness might be cured by medicine. Let us hope that these gentle-men were all properly physicked. I myself have often heard men express similar sentiments of aversion to the feline race ; and sometimes young ladies have done so in my hearing. In both cases I have little doubt but that the weakness is easily overcome. As for a hidden and unheard Cat's presence affecting a person's nerves, I beg to state my conviction that such a story is utterly ridiculous ; and I was vastly entertained by the following narrative, written by a lady for a Magazine for Boys, and given as a truth. Such a valuable fact in natural history should not be allowed to perish ; she calls it, A TALE OF MY GRANDMOTHER.

My maternal grandmother had so strong an aversion to Cats that it seemed to endow her with an additional sense. You may, perhaps, have heard people use the phrase, that they were "frightened out of their seven senses," without troubling yourselves to wonder how they came to have more than *five.* But the Druids of old used to include sympathy and antipathy in the number, a belief which has, no doubt, left its trace in the above popular and otherwise unmeaning expression ; and this extra sense of antipathy my grandmother certainly exhibited as regarding Cats.

When she was a young and pretty little bride, dinner parties and routs, as is usual on such occasions, were given in her honour. In those days, now about eighty years ago, people usually dined early in the afternoon, and you may imagine somewhere in Yorkshire, a large company assembled for a grand dinner by daylight. With all due decorum and old-fashioned stately politeness, the ladies in rustling silks, stately hoops, and nodding plumes, are led to their seats by their respective cavaliers, in bright coloured coats with large gilt buttons.

With dignified bows and profound curtsies, they take their places, the bride, of course, at her host's right hand. The bustle subsides, the servants remove the covers, the carving-knives are brandished by experienced hands, and the host having made the first incision in a goodly sirloin or haunch, turns to enquire how his fair guest wishes to be helped.

To his surprise, he beholds her pretty face flushed and uneasy, while she lifts the snowy damask and looks beneath the table.

" What is the matter, my dear madam ? Have you lost something ? "

" No, sir, nothing, thank you ; — it is the *Cat*," replied the timid bride, with a slight shudder, as she pronounced the word.

" The Cat ? " echoed the gentleman, with a puzzled

smile ; " but, my dear Mrs. H—, we have no Cat !"

" Indeed ! that is very odd, for there is certainly a Cat in the room."

" Did you see it then ? "

" No, sir, no : I did not *see* it, but I *know* it is in the room."

" Do you fancy you heard one then ? "

" No, sir."

" What is the matter, my dear ? " now enquires the lady of the house, from the end of the long table ; " the dinner will be quite cold while you are talking to your fair neighbour so busily."

" Mrs. H— says there is a Cat in the room, my love ; but we have no Cat, have we ? "

" No, certainly ! " replied the lady tartly. " Do carve the haunch, Mr.—."

The footman held the plate nearer, a due portion of the savoury meat was placed upon it.

" To Mrs. H—," said the host, and turned to look again at his fair neighbour ; but her uneasiness and confusion were greater than ever. Her brow was crimson — every eye was turned towards her, and she looked ready to cry.

" I will leave the room, if you will allow me, sir, for I *know* that there is a Cat in the room."

" But, my dear madam—"

" I am quite sure there is, sir ; I *feel* it—I would rather go."

" John, Thomas, Joseph, *can* there be a Cat in the room ? " demanded the embarrassed host of the servants.

" Quite impossible, sir ; — have not seen such a hanimal about the place since I comed, any way."

" Well, look under the table, at any rate ; the lady says she *feels* it ; look in every corner of the room, and let us try to convince her."

" My dear, my dear ! " remonstrated the annoyed bridegroom from a distant part of the table ; "what trouble you are giving."

" Indeed, I would rather leave the room," said the little bride, slipping from her chair. But, meanwhile, the servants ostentatiously bustled in their unwilling search for what they believed to be a phantom fancy of the young lady's brain ; when, lo ! one of the footmen took hold of a half-closed window-shutter, and from the aperture behind out sprang a large cat into the midst of the astonished circle, eliciting cries and exclamations from others than the finely organised bride, who clasped her hands rigidly, and gasped with pallid lips.

Such facts as this are curious, certainly, and remain a puzzle to philosophers.

This habit of hiding itself in secret places is one of the most unpleasant characteristics of the Cat. I know many instances of it—especially of a night alarm when we were children, ending in a strange cat being found in a clothes bag.

Here, indeed, we have truth several degrees stranger than fiction; but this is not the only wonderful story the authoress has to tell. I will give you some others very slightly abridged.

" A year or two ago, a man in the south of Ireland severely chastised his cat for some misdemeanour, immediately after which the animal stole away, and was seen no more.

" A few days subsequently, as this man was starting to go from home, the Cat met and stood before him in a narrow path, with rather a wicked aspect. Its owner slashed his handkerchief at her to frighten her out of the way, but the Cat, undismayed, sprang at the hand, and held it with so ferocious a gripe, that it was impossible to make it open its jaws, and the creature's body had actually to be cut from the head, and the jaws afterwards to be severed, before the mangled hand could be extricated. The man died from the injuries."

The jaws of a Cat are comparatively strong, and worked by powerful muscles ; it has thirty-four teeth, but they are for the most part very tiny teeth, like pin's points. What, I wonder, were the dimensions of this ferocious animal with the iron jaws ; and how many courageous souls were engaged in its destruction. If this story is, however, rather hard to swallow, the next is not less so. Says our authoress—

" I also know an Irish gentleman, who being an only son without any playmates, was allowed, when he was a child, to have a whole family of Cats sleeping in the bed with him every night.

" One day he had beaten the father of the family for some offence, and when he was asleep at night, the revengeful beast seized him by the throat, and would probably have killed him had not instant help been at hand. "The Cat sprang from the window, and was never more seen." (Probably went away in a flash of blue fire.)

What do you think of these very strange stories ? If they surprise you, however, what will you say to this one ? " Dr. C—, an Italian gentleman still living in Florence (the initial is just a little un-satisfactory), who knew at least one of the parties, related to the authoress the following singular story.

A certain country priest in Tuscany, who lived quite alone with his servants, naturally attached himself, in the want of better society, to a fine he-cat, which sat by his stove in winter, and always ate from his plate.

One day a brother priest was the good man's guest, and, in the rare enjoyment of genial conversation, the Cat was neglected; resenting this, he attempted to help himself from his master's plate, instead of waiting for the special morsels which were usually placed on the margin for his use, and was requited with a sharp rap on the head for the liberty. This excited the animal's indignation still more, and springing from the table with an angry cry, he darted to the other side of the room. The two priests thought no more of the Cat until the cloth was about to be removed; when the master of the house prepared a plateful of scraps for his forward favourite, and called him by name to come and enjoy his share of the feast. No joyful Cat obeyed the familiar call: his master observed him looking sulkily from the recess of the window, and rose, holding out the plate, and calling to him in a caressing voice. As he did not approach, however, the old gentleman put the platter aside, saying he might please himself, and sulk instead of dine, if he preferred it ; and then resumed his conversation with his friend. A little later the old gentleman showed symptoms of drowsiness, so his visitor begged that he would not be on ceremony with him, but lie down and take the nap which he knew he was accustomed to indulge in after dinner, and he in the meantime would stroll in the garden for an hour. This was agreed to. The host stretched himself on a couch, and threw his handkerchief over his face to protect him from the summer flies, while the guest stepped through a French window which opened on a terrace and shrubbery.

An hour or somewhat more had passed when he returned, and found his friend still recumbent : he did not at first think of disturbing him, but after a few minutes, considering that he had slept very long, he looked more observantly towards the couch, and was struck by the perfect immobility of the figure, and with something peculiar in the position of the head over which the handkerchief lay disordered. Approaching nearer he saw that it was stained with blood, and hastily removing it, saw, to his unutterable horror, that his poor friend's throat was gashed across, and that life was already extinct.

He started back, shocked and dismayed, and for

a few moments remained gazing on the dreadful
spectacle almost paralysed. Then came the specu-
lation who could have done so cruel a deed? An
old man murdered sleeping—a good man, beloved
by his parishioners and scarcely known beyond the
narrow circle of his rural home. It was his duty to
investigate the mystery, so he composed his countenance as well as he was able, and going to the
door of the room, called for a servant.

The man who had waited at table presently appeared, rubbing his eyes, for he, too, had been
asleep.

" Tell me who has been into this room while I
was in the garden."

" Nobody, your reverence ; no one ever disturbs
the master during his siesta."

He then asked the servant where he had been, and
was told in the' ante-room. He next enquired
whether any person had been in or out of the house,
or if he had heard any movement or voice in the
room, and also how many fellow-servants the man
had. He was told that he had heard no noise or
voices, and that he had two fellow-servants—the
cook and a little boy. His reverence demanded
that they should be brought in, that he might
question them.

They came, and were cross-questioned as closely as possible, but they declared that they had not been in that part of the house all day long, and that nobody could possibly get into the house without their knowledge, unless it was through the garden. The priest had been walking all the time in view of the house, and he felt convinced that the murderer could not have passed in or out on that side without his knowledge.

" Listen to me ; some person has been into that room since dinner, and your master is cruelly murdered."

" Murdered !" cried the three domestics in tones of terror and amazement ; "did your reverence say 'murdered'? "

" He lies where I left him, but his throat is gashed from ear to ear—he is dead. My poor old friend !"

" Dead ! the poor master dead, murdered in his own house."

They wrung their hands, tore their hair, and wept aloud.

" Silence ! I command you ; and consider that every one of us standing here is liable to the suspicion of complicity in this foul deed ; so look to it. Giuseppe was asleep."

" But I sleep very lightly, your reverence."

" Come in and see your master," said the priest solemnly.

They crept in, white with fear and stepping noiselessly. They gazed on the shocking spectacle transfixed with horror. Then a cry of " Who can have done it ?" burst from all lips.

" Who, indeed ?" repeated the cook.

The priest desired Giuseppe to look round the premises, and count the plate, and ascertain if there had been a robbery, or if any one was concealed about the house. The man returned without throwing any new light upon the mystery ; but, in his absence, while surveying the room more carefully than he had previously done, the priest's eye met those of the Cat glowing like lurid flames, as he sat crouching in the shade near a curtain. The orbs had a fierce malignant expression, which startled him, and at once recalled to his recollection the angry and sullen demeanour of the creature during dinner.

" Could it possibly be the Cat that killed him ?" demanded of the cook the awe-struck priest.

" Who knows ?" replied he ; " the beast was surly to others, but always seemed to love him fondly ; and then the wound seems as though it were made with a weapon."

A TALE OF TERROR.

Page 29.

" It does, certainly," rejoined the priest ; " yet I mistrust that brute, and we will try to put it to the proof, at any rate."

After many suggestions, they agreed to pass cords round the neck and under the shoulders of the deceased, and carried the ends outside the room door, which was exactly opposite the couch where he lay. They then all quietly left the apartment, almost closing the door, and remained perfectly still.

One of the party was directed to keep his eye fixed on the Cat, the others after a short delay slowly pulled the cords, which had the effect of partially raising the head of the corpse.

Instantly, at this apparent sign of life, the savage Cat sprang from its corner, and, with a low yell and a single bound, fastened upon the mangled neck of its victim.

At once the sad mystery was solved, the treacherous, ungrateful, cowardly, and revengeful murderer discovered ! and all that remained to be done was to summon help to destroy the wild beast, and in due time to bury the good man in peace.

Well, to such stories as these I have no particular objection, under certain circumstances. They are

well enough, for instance, to fill up the odd corners
of a weekly newspaper in the dull season, and are a
pleasant relief to the 'enormous gooseberry'; but I
have my doubts whether they should be given as
facts for the instruction of youth, though I am not
much surprised that the editor should have ad-
mitted them into his pages, when he speaks of them
in another part of the magazine as "delightful
papers." When children's minds are thus filled
with absurd falsehoods, it is not to be wondered at
if, when the child grows up into a man, the man
should express himself somewhat in the words of
this instructor of youth, who says, "I must confess,
on my own part, an aversion. to the feline race,
which, with the best intentions, I am unable entirely
to conquer. I have occasionally become rather
fond of an individual Cat, but never encounter one,
unexpectedly, without a feeling of repugnance; and,
as I like, or feel an interest in, every other animal,
I regard this peculiarity as hereditary."

I suppose, however, that there are few of my
fair readers who have not a feeling somewhat akin
to repugnance towards snakes, black-beetles, earwigs,
spiders, rats, and even poor little, harmless mice;
yet ladies have been known to keep white mice, and
make pets of them after a time, when the first

timidity was overcome. There was a captive once, you may remember, who tamed a spider. A man, about ten years ago, who used to go about the streets, got his living by pretending to swallow snakes. He allowed them, while holding tight on their tails, to crawl half-way down his throat and back again. He said they were nice clean animals, and good company. Little boys at school often swallow frogs. An earwig probably has fine social qualities, which only want bringing out : naturalists tell us they make the best of mothers. The black beetle has always been a maligned insect : it is a sort of nigger among insects, apparently born only to be poisoned, drowned, or smashed ; but some one ought, decidedly, to take the race in hand and see of what it is capable. I have, myself, a horror of most of the creatures I have named, but happen not to have been reared with an aversion for Cats, and I have a strong belief that if I tried hard (which I am not going to do) I might get upon friendly relations with the other animals named above, which, I suppose, most of us are taught, when children, to dislike; and as our fathers and mothers have entertained the same feeling, perhaps, as my authoress says, we may "regard this peculiarity as hereditary."

Probably a good many ladies reading these lines will endorse my authoress's opinions. For the most part these will be married ladies with large families ; and it will be found upon enquiry, I feel certain, that ladies who have many children will have a dislike for the feline race.

CHAPTER III.

D

CHAPTER III.

—o—

*Of other Wicked Stories, with a
few Words in Defence of the
Accused.*

—o—

I TOLD you a-
while ago what
good Mr. Mavor
says of Cats.
" La défiance que cet animal inspire," says another
instructor of youth, M. Pujoulx, in his *Livre du
Second Age*, " est bien propre à corriger de dissimulation et de l'hypocrisie." I have nothing to say of
poor Pujoulx, whose books and opinions are by this
time well nigh forgotten ; but what am I to think
of two other authors, whose words should be law,

but of the value of which I leave you to judge for
yourself. I need not, I think, remind you that
there is a natural history written by one Monsieur
Buffon, "containing a theory of the earth, a general
history of man, of the brute creation, and of vege-
tables, minerals, etc.," of which Mr. Barr published
an English translation in ten goodly volumes.
Thus, in this work of world-wide celebrity, is the
feline race discussed. I give the author's words as
I find them :—

"The Cat is a faithless domestic, and only kept
through necessity to oppose to another domestic
which incommodes us still more, and which we cannot drive away ; for we pay no respect to those,
who, being fond of all beasts, keep Cats for amusement. Though these animals are gentle and
frolicksome when young, yet they, even then,
possess an innate cunning and perverse disposition,
which age increases, and which education only
serves to conceal. They are, naturally, inclined to
theft, and the best education only converts them
into servile and flattering robbers ; for they have
the same address, subtlety, and inclination for
mischief or rapine. Like all knaves, they know
how to conceal their intentions, to watch, wait, and
choose opportunities for seizing their prey ; to fly

from punishment, and to remain away until the danger is over, and they can return with safety. They readily conform to the habits of society, but never acquire its manners ; for of attachment they have only the appearance, as may be seen by the obliquity of their motions, and duplicity of their looks. They never look in the face those who treat them best, and of whom they seem to be the most fond ; but either through fear or falsehood, they approach him by windings to seek for those caresses they have no pleasure in, but only to flatter those from whom they receive them. Very different from that faithful animal the dog, whose sentiments are all directed to the person of his master, the Cat appears only to feel for himself, only to love conditionally, only to partake of society that he may abuse it ; and by this disposition he has more affinity to man than the dog, who is all sincerity."

So much for M. Buffon : though he is sadly mistaken on the subject of which he writes, these were probably his honest opinions ; but what can be said for a writer in the Encyclopædia Britannica, who holds forth as follows, and is not only ignorant of what he talks about, but steals Buffon's absurd prejudices, and passes them off as his own. In his opinion the cat "is a useful but deceitful domestic. Although when young it is playful and gay, it possesses at the same time an innate malice and perverse disposition, which increases as it grows up, and which education learns it to conceal, but never to subdue. Constantly bent upon theft and rapine, though in a domestic state, it is full of cunning and dissimulation : it conceals all its designs, seizes every opportunity of doing mischief, and then flies from punishment. It easily takes on the habits of society, but never its manners ; for it has only the appearance of friendship and attachment. This disingenuity of character is betrayed by the obliquity of its movements and the ambiguity of its looks. In a word, the Cat is totally destitute of friendship."

Here, I think, are some pretty sentiments and some valuable information about the Cat-kind. Let us hope that the other contributors to the Encyclopædia knew something more of what they wrote about than the gentleman above quoted. And these opinions are not uncommon ; for instance, allow me to quote from an article in a popular miscellany :—

"No! I cannot abide Cats," says the writer. "Pet Cats, wild Cats, Tom Cats, gib Cats, Persian

Cats, Angora Cats, tortoiseshell Cats, tabby Cats,
black Cats, Manx Cats, brindled Cats, mewing
once, twice, or thrice, as the case may be,—none of
these Cats delight me ; they are associated in my
mind with none but disagreeable objects and re-
membrances—old maids, witchcraft, dreadful sab-
baths, with old women flying up the chimney
upon broom-sticks, to drink hell-broth with the evil
one, charms, incantations, sorceries, sucking children's breaths, stopping out late on the tiles, catter-
wauling and molrowing in the night season, prowling about the streets at unseasonable hours, and a
variety of other things, too numerous and too unpleasant to mention."

Upon the other hand, Puss has had her defenders,
and Miss Isabel Hill writes thus :—

" Poor Pinkey, I can scarce dare a word in praise
of one belonging to thy slandered sisterhood ; yet
a few good examples embolden me to assert that I
have rarely known any harm of Cats who were
given a fair chance, though I own I have seldom
met with any that have enjoyed that advantage.
Is it their fault that they are born nearly without
brains, though with all their senses about them, and
of a tender turn ?   That they want strength, both
of body and instinct, are dependant, and ill edu-

cated? No! their errors are thrust upon them; they become selfish per force, cowards from their tenacious regard for that personal neatness which they so labour to preserve. Oh! that all females made such good use of their tongues! Cross from sheer melancholy, reflecting, in their starved and persecuted maturity, on the fondness lavished over the days in which they were pet useless toys; as soon as they can deserve and may require kind treatment, they are as ill-used as if they were constant wives—rather unfair on ladies of their excessive genius. Could every Cat, like Whittington's, catch fortunes for her master as well as mice, we should hear no more said against the species. Suppose they only fawn on us because we house and feed them, they have no nobler proofs of friendship with which to thank us; and if their very gratitude for this self-interested hire be adduced as a crime, alas! poor Pussies! Had Minette been a Thomas, a whiskered fur-collared Philander, he would most probably have surmounted that unmanly weakness, and received all favours as but his due. I never see a Mrs. Mouser rubbing her soft coat against me, with round upturned eyes, but I translate her purr into words like these:—'I can't swim; I can neither fetch and carry, nor guard the house; I can only love you, mistress ; pray accept all I have to offer.' "

An anonymous writer says : " We may learn some useful lessons from Cats, as indeed, from all animals. Agur, in the book of Proverbs, refers to some ; and all through Scripture we find animals used as types of human character. Cats may teach us patience, and perseverance, and earnest concentration of mind on a desired object, as they watch for hours together by a mouse-hole, or in ambush for a bird. In their nicely calculated springs, we are taught neither to come short through want of mercy, or go beyond the mark in its excess. In their delicate walking amidst the fragile articles on a table or mantelpiece, is illustrated the tact and discrimination by which we should thread rather than force our way ; and, in pursuit of our own ends, avoid the injuring of others. In their noiseless tread and stealthy movements, we are reminded of the frequent importance of secresy and caution prior to action, while their promptitude at the right moment, warns us, on the other hand, against the evils of irresolution and delay. The curiosity with which they spy into all places, and the thorough smelling which any new object invariably receives from them, commends to us the pursuit of knowledge, even under diffi-

culties. Cats, however, will never smell the same
thing twice over, thereby showing a retentive as well
as an acquiring faculty. Then to speak of what
may be learned from their mere form and ordinary
motions, so full of beauty and gracefulness. What
Cat was ever awkward or clumsy? Whether in
play or in earnest, Cats are the very embodi-
ment of elegance. As your Cat rubs her head
against something you offer her, which she either
does not fancy or does not want, she instructs you
that there is a gracious mode of refusing a thing ;
and as she sits up like a bear, on her hind legs, to
ask for something (which Cats will often do for a
long time together), you may see the advantage of
a winning and engaging way, as well when you are
seeking a favour as when you think fit to decline
one. If true courtesy and considerateness should
prevent you not merely from positively hurting
another, but also from purposely clashing, say,
with another's fancies, peculiarities, or predilections,
this too, may be learned from the Cat, who does
not like to be rubbed the wrong way (who does like
to be rubbed the wrong way?), and who objects to
your treading on her tail. Nor is the soft foot,
with its skilfully sheathed and ever sharp claws,
without a moral too ; for whilst there is nothing

commendable in anything approaching to spite, passion, or revenge, a character that is all softness is certainly defective. The velvety paw is very well, but it will be the better appreciated when it is known that it carries within it something that is not soft, and which can make itself felt, and sharply felt, on occasion. A cat rolled up into a ball, or crouched with its paws folded underneath it, seems an emblem of repose and contentment. There is something soothing in the mere sight of it. It may remind one of the placid countenance and calm repose with which the sphynx seems to look forth from the shadow of the Pyramids, on the changes and troubles of the world. This leads to the remark, that Cats, after all, are very enigmatical creatures. You never get to the bottom of Cats. You will never find any two, well known to you, that do not offer marked diversities in ways and dispositions; and, in general, the combination they exhibit of activity and repose, and the rapidity with which they pass from the one to the other, their gentle aspects and fragile form, united with strength and pliancy, their sudden appearances and disappearances, their tenacity of life, and many escapes from dangers ("as many lives as a Cat"), their silent and rapid movements, their sometimes unaccountable gatherings, and strange noises at night —all contribute to invest them with a mysterious fascination, which reaches its culminating point in the (not very frequent) case of a completely black cat."

Instances are frequent, I am happy to tell Cat-haters, of illustrious persons who have been attached to the feline race, and of Cats who have merited such attachment.

Mahomet would seem to have been very fond of Cats, for it is said that he once cut off the sleeve of his robe rather than disturb his favourite while sleeping on it. Petrarch was so fond of his Cat that when it died he had it embalmed, and placed in a niche in his apartment; and you ought to read what Rousseau has to say in favour of the feline race. M. Baumgarten tells us that he saw a hospital for Cats at Damascus : it was a large house, walled round very carefully, and said to be full of patients. It was at Damascus that the incident above related occurred to Mahomet. His followers in this place ever afterwards paid a great respect to Cats, and supported the hospital in question by public sub-scriptions with much liberality.

When the Duke of Norfolk was committed to the Tower, in the reign of Queen Elizabeth, a favourite Cat made her way into the prison room by getting down the chimney.

"The first day," says Lady Morgan, in her delightful book, "we had the honour of dining at the palace of the Archbishop of Toronto, at Naples, he said to me, 'You must pardon my passion for Cats, but I never exclude them from my dining-room, and you will find they make excellent company.' Between the first and second course, the door opened, and several enormously large and beautiful Angora Cats were introduced by the names of Pantalone, Desdemona, Otello, etc. : they took their places on chairs near the table, and were as silent, as quiet, as motionless, and as well behaved as the most *bon ton* table in London could require. On the bishop requesting one of the chaplains to help the Signora Desdemona, the butler stepped up to his lordship, and observed, 'My lord, La Signora Desdemona will prefer waiting for the roasts.' "

Gottfried Mind, the celebrated Swiss painter, was called the "Cat Raphael," from the excellence with which he painted that animal. This peculiar talent was discovered and awakened by chance. At the time when Frendenberger painted his picture of the "Peasant Clearing Wood," before his cottage, with his wife sitting by, and feeding her child out of a basin, round which a Cat is prowling, Mind, his new pupil, stared very hard at the sketch of this last figure, and Frendenberger asked with a smile whether he thought he could draw a better. Mind offered to show what he could do, and did draw a Cat, which Frendenberger liked so much that he asked his pupil to elaborate the sketch, and the master copied the scholar's work, for it is Mind's Cat that is engraved in Frendenberger's plate. Prints of Mind's Cats are now common.

Mind did not look upon Cats merely as subjects for art; his liking for them was very great. Once when hydrophobia was raging in Berne, and eight hundred were destroyed in consequence of an order issued by the civic authorities, Mind was in great distress on account of their death. He had, however, successfully hidden his own favourite, and she escaped the slaughter. This Cat was always with him when he worked, and he used to carry on a sort of conversation with her by gesture and signs. It is said that Minette sometimes occupied his lap, while two or three kittens perched on his shoulders; and he was often known to remain for an hour together in almost the same attitude for fear of disturbing them; yet he was generally thought to be a passionate, sour-tempered man. It is said that Cardinal Wolsey used to accommodate his favourite Cat with part of his regal seat when he gave an audience or received princely company.

There is a funny story told of Barrett, the painter, another lover of Cats. He had for pets a Cat and a kitten, its progeny. A friend seeing two holes in the bottom of his door, asked him for what purpose he made them there. Barrett said it was for the Cats to go in and out.

"Why," replied his friend, "would not one do for both?"

"You silly man," answered the painter, "how could the big Cat get into the little hole?"

"But," said his friend, "could not the little one go through the big hole?"

"Dear me," cried Barrett, "so she could; well, I never thought of that."

M. Sonnini had an Angora Cat, of which he writes: "This animal was my principal amusement for several years. How many times have her tender caresses made me forget my troubles, and consoled me in my misfortunes. My beautiful companion at length perished. After several days of suffering,

during which I never forsook her, her eyes constantly
fixed on me, were at length extinguished ; and her
loss rent my heart with sorrow."

You have heard, of course, of Doctor Johnson's
feline favourite, and how it fell ill, and how he,
thinking the servants might neglect it, himself
turned Cat-nurse, and having found out that the
invalid had a fancy for oysters, daily administered
them to poor Pussy until she had quite recovered.
I like to picture to myself that good old grumpy
doctor nursing Pussy on his knee, and wasting who
shall say how many precious moments which otherwise might have been devoted to his literary avo-
cations. I dare say now, in that tavern parlour
where the lexicographer held forth so ably after
sun-set, he made but scant allusion to his nursing
feats, lest some mad wit might have twitted him
upon the subject, for you may be sure that the wits
of those days, as of ours, could have been mighty
satirical on such a theme.

Madame Helvetius had a Cat that used to lie
at its mistress's feet, scarcely ever leaving her for
five minutes together. It would never take food
from any other hand, and it would allow no one but
its mistress to caress it ; but it would obey her
commands in everything, fetching objects she

wanted in its mouth, like a dog. During **Madame**
Helvetius's last illness, the poor animal never quitted
her chamber, and though it was removed after **her**
death, it returned again next morning, and slowly
and mournfully paced to and fro **in the room, crying**
piteously all **the time. Some days after its mis-**
tress's funeral, it was found stretched dead upon
her grave, having, it would **seem,** died of grief.

There is a well-authenticated story **of a Cat**
which **having had a thorn taken out of her foot by a**
man **servant, remembered him, and welcomed him**
with delight when she saw him again after an
absence of two years.

As a strong **instance of attachment, I can quote**
the case of a she Cat of my own, which always
waited **for me** in the passage when **I returned home**
of an **evening,** and mounted **upon my shoulder**
to ride upstairs. Returning home once after **an**
absence of six **weeks, this Cat sat on the corner of**
the mantel-piece, **close by the bed, all** night, and as it
would appear wide awake, keeping **a sort of guard**
over me, for being very restless **I lay awake a long**
while, and then awoke **again,** several times, after
dozing off, to find upon each occasion Miss Puss,
with **wide open eyes, purring loudly. I may add,**
that although, when we have gone away from home,

E

the Cats have taken their meals and spent most of their time with the servants, yet upon our return they have immediately resumed their old ways, and cut the kitchen dead.

By the report of a police case at Marlborough Street, on the 28th of June last, it appeared that a husband, brutally ill-using his wife, flung her on the ground, and seizing her by the throat, endeavoured to strangle her. While, however, she lay thus, a favourite Cat, named "Topsy," suddenly sprang upon the man, and fastened her claws and teeth in his face. He could not tear the Cat away, and was obliged to implore the woman he had been ill-using to take the Cat from him to save his life.

The Cat is reproached with treachery and cruelty, but Bigland argues that the artifices which it uses are the particular instincts which the all-wise Creator has given it, in conformity with the purposes for which it was designed. Being destined to prey upon a lively and active animal like the mouse, which possesses so many means of escape, it is requisite that it should be artful ; and, indeed, the Cat, when well observed, exhibits the most evident proofs of a particular adaptation to a particular purpose, and the most striking example of a peculiar instinct suited to its destiny.

Every animal has its own way of killing and eating its prey. The fox leaves the legs and hinder parts of a hare or rabbit ; the weasel and stoat eat the brains, and nibble about the head, and suck the blood ; crows and magpies peck at the eyes ; the dog tears his prey to pieces indiscriminately ; the Cat always turns the skin inside out like a glove.

Mr. Buckland relates the case of a gamekeeper who bought up all the Cats in the neighbouring town, cut off their heads, and nailed them up as trophies of veritable captures in the woods. In a gamekeeper's museum, visited by the same writer, were no less than fifty-three Cats' heads staring hideously down from the shelves. There was a story attached to each head. One Cat was killed in such a wood ; another in such a hedge-row ; some in traps, some shot, some knocked on the head with a stick ; but what was most remarkable was the different expression of countenance observable in each individual head. One had died fighting desperately to the last, and giving up its nine lives inch by inch. Caught in a trap, it had lingered the night through in dreadful agony, the pain of its entrapped limb causing it to make furious efforts to free itself, each effort but lending another torment to the wound.

In the morning the gamekeeper had released the poor exhausted creature for the dogs to worry out what little life was left in its body.   The head dried by the heat of two summers, the wrinkled forehead, the expanded eyelids, the glary eyeballs, the whiskers stretched to their full extent, the spiteful lips, exposing the double row of tiger-like teeth, envenomed by agony, told all this.   The hand of death had not been powerful enough to relax the muscles racked for so many hours of pain and terror.

Another Cat's head wore a very different expression ; she had neither been worried nor tortured. Creeping, stealthily, on the tips of her beautifully padded feet, behind some overhanging hedge, the hidden gamekeeper had suddenly shot her dead. In death her face was calm ; no expression of fear ruffled her features ; she had been shot down and died instantly at the moment of anticipated triumph.

A third head belonged to a poor little Puss that had died before it had attained the age of cathood ; her young life had been knocked out of her with a stick : her head still retained the kitten's playful look, and there was an appealing expression about it as though it had died quickly, wondering in what it had done wrong.

I find a writer upon Cats who speaks thus in their praise :—

"It has been said that the Cat is one of those animals which has made the least return to man for his trouble by its services ; but it is certain that it renders very essential service to man."

And another says :—

"Authors seem to delight in exaggerating the good qualities of the Dog, while they depreciate those of the Cat ; the latter, however, is not less useful, and certainly less mischievous, than the former."

Indeed, it would be unfair not to state that Pussy has had many able defenders, who have argued her case in verse as well as prose ; for example, in Edmond Moore's fable of "*The Farmer, the Spaniel and the Cat*," the Spaniel, when Puss drew near to eat some of the fragments of a feast, repelled her, saying she does nothing to merit being fed, etc. :—

> " ' I own' (with meekness Puss replied)
> ' Superior merit on your side ;
> Nor does my breast with envy swell
> To find it recompens'd so well.
> Yet I, in what my nature can,
> Contribute to the good of man.
> Whose claws destroy the pilf'ring mouse ?
> Who drives the vermin from the house ?

> Or, watchful for the lab'ring swain,
> From lurking rats secures the grain?
> For this, if he rewards bestow,
> Why should your heart with gall o'erflow?
> Why pine my happiness to see,
> Since there's enough for you and me?'
> ' Thy words are just,' the Farmer cried,
> And spurned the Spaniel from his side."

And, again, the same idea occurs in Gay's fable of the " *Man, the Cat, the Dog, and the Fly.*" The Cat solicits aid from the Man in the social state.

> " ' Well, Puss,' says Man, 'and what can you
> To benefit the public do?'
> The Cat replies, ' These teeth, these claws,
> With vigilance shall serve the cause.
> The Mouse, destroy'd by my pursuit,
> No longer shall your feasts pollute;
> Nor Rats, from nightly ambuscade,
> With wasteful teeth your stores invade.
> ' I grant,' says Man, ' to general use
> Your parts and talents may conduce;
> For rats and mice purloin our grain,
> And threshers whirl the flail in vain;
> Thus shall the Cat, a foe to spoil,
> Protect the farmers' honest toil.' "

Mr. Ruskin says, "There is in every animal's eye a dim image and gleam of humanity, a flash of strange life through which their life looks at and up to our great mystery of command over them, and claims the fellowship of the creature, if not of the soul !"

Poor Pussy ! on the whole she has had but few champions in comparison to the number of her foes. Let us see what anecdotes we can find which will show her in a favourable light ; but my chapter is long enough, and I will conclude it with the epitaph placed over a favourite French Puss :—

" Ci repose pauvre Mouton,
Qui jamais ne fût glouton ;
J'espère bien que le roi Pluton,
Lui donnera bon gîte et crouton."

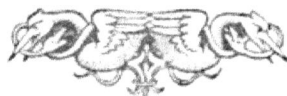

CHAPTER IV.

CHAPTER IV.

—o—

*Of the Manners and Customs of
Cats.*

—o—

ET us see
though, before
we try our anec-
dotes, what is
known of the Cat's pecu-
liarities. I rather like
this quaint description of the domestic Pussy, which
occurs in an old heraldic book, John Bossewell's
" *Workes of Armorie*," published in 1597 :—

" The field is of the Saphire, on a chief Pearle, a
Masion Cruieves. This beaste is called a ' Masion,'
for that he is enimie to Myse and Rattes. He is

slye and wittie, and seeth so sharpely that he over-
commeth darkness of the nighte by the shyninge
lyghte of his eyne. In shape of body he is like
unto a Leoparde, and hathe a greate mouthe. He
doth delighte that he enjoyeth his libertie; and in
his youth he is swifte, plyante, and merye. He
maketh a rufull noyse and a gastefulle when he pro-
fereth to fighte with another. He is a cruell beaste
when he is wilde, and falleth on his owne feete
from moste highe places: and never is hurt there-
with. When he hathe a fayre skinne, he is, as it
were, proude thereof, and then he goethe muche
aboute to be seene."

It is commonly supposed that a Cat's scratch is
venomous, because a lacerated wound oftener fes-
ters than a smooth cut from a sharp knife.

It is erroneously said that Cats feel a cutaneous
irritation at the approach of rain, and offer sensible
evidence of uneasiness: allusion may be found to
this in "Thomson's Seasons." Virgil has also made
the subject a theme for poetic allusion.

The Chinese look into their Cat's eyes to know
what o'clock it is; and the playfulness of Cats is
said to indicate the coming of a storm. I have
noticed this often myself, and have seen them rush
about in a half wild state just before windy weather.

I think it is when the wind is *rising* that they are most affected.

It is stated in a Japanese book that the tip of a Cat's nose is always cold, except on the day corresponding with our Midsummer-day. This is a question I cannot say I have gone into deeply. I know, however, that Cats always have a warm nose when they first awaken from sleep. All Cats are fond of warmth. I knew one which used to open an oven door after the kitchen fire was out, and creep into the oven. One day the servant shut the door, not noticing the Cat was inside, and lighted the fire. For a long while she could not make out whence came the sounds of its crying and scratching, but fortunately made the discovery in time to save its life. A Cat's love of the sunshine is well known, and perhaps this story may not be unfamiliar to the reader :—

One broiling hot summer's day Charles James Fox and the Prince of Wales were lounging up St. James's street, and Fox laid the Prince a wager that he would see more Cats than his Royal Highness during their promenade, although the Prince might choose which side of the street he thought fit. On reaching Piccadilly, it turned out that Fox had seen thirteen Cats and the Prince none. The

Prince asked for an explanation of this apparent miracle.

"Your Royal Highness," said Fox, "chose, of course, the shady side of the way as most agreeable. I knew that the sunny side would be left for me, and that Cats prefer the sunshine."

Cats usually, but not always, fall on their feet, because of the facility with which they balance themselves when springing from a height, which power of balancing is in some degree produced by the flexibility of the heel, the bones of which have no fewer than four joints. Cats alight softly on their feet, because in the middle of the foot is a large ball or pad in five parts, formed of an elastic substance, and at the base of each toe is a similar pad. No mechanism better calculated to break the force of a fall could be imagined.

A Cat, when falling with its head downwards, curls its body, so that the back forms an arch, while the legs remain extended. This so changes the position of the centre of gravity, that the body makes a half turn in the air, and the feet become lowest.

In the inside of a Cat's head there is a sort of partition wall projecting from the sides, a good way inwards, towards the centre, so as to prevent the brain from suffering from concussion.

There is a breed of tail-less white Cats in the Isle of Man, and also in Devonshire. These are not the sort of animals with which, on shipboard, the "stow-aways" are made acquainted.

A great many Cats in the Isle of Man are said to be deaf. Thus, "As deaf as a Manx Cat." There is an idea that white Cats with blue eyes are always deaf, but a correspondent of *Notes and Queries* says, " I am myself possessed of a white Cat which, at the advanced age of upwards of seventeen years, still retains its hearing to great perfection, and is remarkably intelligent and devoted, more so than Cats are usually given credit for. Its affection for persons is, indeed, more like that of a dog than of a Cat. It is a half-bred Persian Cat, and its eyes are perfectly blue, with round pupils, not elongated, as those of Cats usually are. It occasionally suffers from irritation in the ears, but this has not at all resulted in deafness."

Do you know why Cats always wash themselves after a meal ? A Cat caught a sparrow, and was about to devour it, but the sparrow said,

" No gentleman eats till he has first washed his face."

The Cat, struck with this remark, set the sparrow down, and began to wash his face with his paw, but the sparrow flew away. This vexed Pussy extremely, and he said,

" As long as I live I will eat first and wash my face afterwards."

Which all Cats do, even to this day.

A French writer says, the three animals that waste most time over their toilet are cats, flies, and women.

The attitudes and motions of a Cat are very graceful, because she is furnished with collar-bones. She can, therefore, carry food to her mouth like a monkey, can clasp, can climb, and can strike sideways, and seat herself at a height upon a very narrow space.

The lateral movements of the head in Cats are not so extensive as in the owl, but are, nevertheless, considerable. A cat can look round pretty far behind it without moving its body, which might be apt to startle its prey. The spine of the Cat is very full and loose, in order that all its movements in all possible directions and circumstances may be free and unrestrained. For this purpose, too, all the joints which connect its bones together are extremely loose and free. Thus, the Cat is enabled to get through small apertures, to leap from great heights, and even to fall in an unfavourable posture with little or no injury to itself. Its ears are not so moveable as those of some other animals, but are more so than in very many animals. The shape of the external ear, or rather cartilaginous portion, is admirably adapted to intercept sounds. The natural posture is forward and outward, so as to catch sounds proceeding from the front and sides. The upper half, however, is moveable, and by means of a thin layer of muscular fibres, it is made to curve backwards and receive sounds from the rear. Although a Cat cannot lick its face and head, it nevertheless cleans these parts thoroughly ; in fact, as we often observe, a Cat licks its right paw for a long time, and then brushes down the corresponding side of the head and face ; and when this is accomplished, it does the same with the other paw and corresponding side.

"'A May kitten makes a dirty Cat,' is a piece of Huntingdonshire folk-lore," says Mr. Cuthbert Bede, "quoted to me in order to deter me from keeping a kitten that had been born in May."

Dr. Turton says, "The Cat has a more voluminous and expressive vocabulary than any other brute ; the short twitter of complacency and affection, the purr of tranquility and pleasure, the mew of distress, the growl of anger, and the horrible

F

wailing of pain." For myself, I seldom hear a
catawauling without thinking of that droll picture
in *Punch* of the old lady sitting up in bed and
pricking up her ears to the music of a mewing
Cat.

"Oh, ah! yes, it's the waits," says she, with a
delighted chuckle; "I love to listen to 'em. It
may be fancy, but somehow they don't seem to
play so sweetly as they did when I was a girl.
Perhaps it is that I am getting old, and don't hear
quite so well as I used to do."

Few, even amongst Pussy's most ardent admirers,
who possess the faculty of hearing, and have heard
the music of Cats, would desire the continuance of
their "sweet voices"; yet a concert was exhibited
at Paris, wherein Cats were the performers. They
were placed in rows, and a monkey beat time to
them, as the Cats mewed; and the historian of the
facts relates that the diversity of the tones which
they emitted produced a very ludicrous effect.
This exhibition was announced to the Parisian
public by the title of "Concert Miaulant."

This would seem to prove that Cats may be
taught tricks, which is not generally believed, but
is nevertheless the case.

In Pool's *Twists and Turns about the Streets of*

London, mention is made of "a poor half-naked boy, strumming a violin, while another urchin with a whip makes two half-starved Cats go through numerous feats of agility."

De Roget says, that in animals that graze and keep their heads for a long time in a dependent position, the danger from an excessive impetus in the blood flowing towards the head is much greater than in other animals ; and we find that an extra-ordinary provision is made to obviate this danger. The arteries which supply the brain on their en-trance into the basis of the skull suddenly divide into a great number of minute branches, forming a complicated network of vessels, an arrangement which, on the well known principle of hydraulics, must greatly check the velocity of the blood con-ducted through them. That such is the real pur-pose of this structure, which has been called the *rete mirabile,* is evident from the branches afterwards uniting into larger trunks when they have entered the brain, through the substance of which they are then distributed exactly as in other animals, where no such previous subdivision takes place. The rete mirabile is much developed in the sheep, but scarcely perceptible in the Cat.

Being an animal which hunts both by day and

night, the structure of its visual organs is adjusted for both. The retina, or expansion of the optic nerve, is most sensitive to the stimulus of light; hence, a well-marked ciliary muscle contracts the pupil to a mere vertical fissure during the day, while in the dark, the pupil dilates enormously, and lets in as much light as possible. But even this would be insufficient, for Cats have to look for their prey in holes, cellars, and other places where little or no light can penetrate. Hence, the Cat is furnished with a bright metal-like, lustrous, membrane, called the *Tapetum*, which lines part of the hollow globe of the eye, and sheds considerable light on the image of an object thrown on the retina. This membrane is, we are told, common to all vertebrated animals, but is especially beautiful and lustrous in nocturnal animals. The herbivora, such as the ox and sheep, have the *tapetum* of the finest enamelled green colour, provided probably to suit the nature of their food, which is green. The subject, however, of the various colours of the *tapetum* in different animals is not yet understood. The sensibility of the retina in Cats is so great that neither the contractions of the pupil nor the closing of the eye-lids would alone afford them sufficient protection from the action of the light. Hence, in common with most animals, the Cat is furnished with a nictitating membrane, which is, in fact, a third eyelid, sliding over the transparent cornea beneath the common eyelids. This membrane is not altogether opaque, but translucent, allowing light to fall on the retina, and acting, as it were, like a shade. The nictitating membrane is often seen in the Cat when she slowly opens her eyes from a calm and prolonged sleep : it is well developed in the eagle, and enables him to gaze steadfastly on the sun's unclouded disk.

The illumination of a Cat's eye in the dark arises from the external light collected on the eye and reflected from it. Although apparently dark, a room is penetrated by imperceptible rays of external light from lamps or other luminiferous bodies. When these rays reach the observer direct, he sees the lamps or luminiferous bodies themselves, but when he is out of their direct sight, the brightness of their illumination only becomes apparent, through the rays being collected and reflected by some appropriate substance.

The cornea of the eye of the Cat, and of many other animals, has a great power of concentrating the rays and reflecting them through the pupil. Professor Bohn, at Leipsic, made experiments

proving that when the external light is wholly
excluded, none can be seen in the Cat's eye. For
the same reason, the animal, by a change of posture or other means, intercepting the rays, immediately deprives the observer of all light otherwise
existing in, or permeating, the room. In this action,
when the iris of the eye is completely open, the
degree of brilliancy is the greatest; but when the
iris is partly contracted, which it always is when
the external light, or the light in the room, is increased, then the illumination is more obscure.
The internal motions of the animals have also great
influence over this luminous appearance, by the
contraction and relaxation of the iris dependent
upon them. When the animal is alarmed, or first
disturbed, it naturally dilates the pupil, and the
eye glares; when it is appeased or composed, the
pupil contracts, and the light in the eye is no
longer seen.

A German savant says, that at the end of each
hair of a Cat's whiskers is a sort of bulb of nervous
substance, which converts it into a most sensitive
feeler. The whiskers are of the greatest use to
her when hunting in the dark. The nervous bulbs
at the ends of a lion's whiskers are as large as a
small pea.

But an English writer differs from him ; thus :—
" Every one must have observed what are usually
called the "whiskers" on a Cat's upper lip. The
use of these, in a state of nature, is very important.
They are organs of touch ; they are attached to a
bed of close glands under the skin ; and each of
these long and stiff hairs is connected with the
nerves of the lip. The slightest contact of these
whiskers with any surrounding object is thus felt
most distinctly by the animal, although the hairs
are of themselves insensible. They stand out on
each side in the lion, as well as in the common
Cat ; so that, from point to point, they are equal
in width to the animal's body. If we imagine,
therefore, a lion stealing through a covert of wood
in an imperfect light, we shall at once see the use
of these long hairs. They indicate to him, through
the nicest feeling, any obstacle which may present
itself to the passage of the body : they prevent the
rustle of boughs and leaves, which would give
warning to his prey if he were to attempt to pass
through too dense a bush, and this, in conjunction
with the soft cushions of his feet, and the fur upon
which he treads (the retractable claws never coming in contact with the ground), enable him to
move towards his victim with a stillness even

greater than that of the snake, who creeps along the grass, and is not perceived till he is coiled round his prey."

Black Cats especially are said to be highly charged with electricity, which, when the animal is irritated, is easily visible in the dark. Here are directions I have for producing the effect :—Lay one hand upon the Cat's throat, and slightly press its shoulder bones. If the other hand be drawn gently along its back, electric shocks will be felt in the hand upon the Cat's throat. If the tips of the ears be touched after the back has been rubbed, shocks of electricity may also be felt, or they may be obtained from the foot. Lay the animal upon your knees, and apply the right hand to the back, the left fore paw resting on the palm of your left hand, apply the thumb to the upper side of the paw, so as to extend the claws, and by this means bring your fore finger in contact with one of the bones of the leg, where it joins the paw ; when from the knob or end of this bone, the finger slightly pressing on it, you may feel distinctly successive shocks similar to those obtained from the ears. The Reverend Mr. Wood expresses an opinion, that on account of the superabundance of electricity which is developed in the Cat, the animal is found very useful to paralysed persons, who instinctively encourage its approach, and from the touch derive some benefit. Those who suffer from rheumatism often find the presence of a Cat alleviate their sufferings. The same gentleman, writing of a favourite Cat, says, that if a hair of her mistress's head were laid upon the animal's back it would writhe as though in agony, and rolling on the floor, would strive to free herself from the object of her fears. The pointing of a finger at her side, at a distance of half a foot, would cause her fur to bristle up and throw her into a violent tremour.

It is difficult to account for the fondness of Cats for fish, as nature seems to have given them an appetite, which, with their great antipathy to water, they can rarely gratify unassisted. Many instances have, however, been recorded of Cats catching fish. A Mr. Moody, of Sesmond, near Newcastle-upon-Tyne, had a Cat in 1829 which had been in his possession for some years, and caught fish with great assiduity, and frequently brought them home alive. Besides minnows and eels, she occasionally carried home pilchards, one of which, about six inches long, was once found in her possession ; she also contrived to teach a neighbour's Cat to fish, and the two were sometimes seen together watching by a river side for their prey.　At other times they were seen at opposite sides of the river, not far from each other, on the look out for game.

A writer in the *Plymouth Journal*, June 1828, says :—" There is now at the battery, on the Devil's Point, a Cat which is an expert catcher of the finny tribe, being in the constant habit of diving into the sea and bringing up the fish alive in her mouth, and depositing them in the guard room for the use of the sailors.　She is now seven years old, and has long been a useful caterer.　It is supposed that her pursuit of the water-rats first taught her to venture into the water, to which it is well known Puss has a natural aversion.　She is now as fond of the water as a Newfoundland dog, and takes her regular peregrinations along the rocks at its edge, looking out for her game ready to dive for it at a moment's notice."

Talking of the Cat's fondness for fish, I should, however, mention, that if a plate of meat and a plate of fish, either raw or cooked, be placed before the generality of Cats, they will be found almost always to choose the meat.

It is usually supposed that a tortoiseshell Tom is an impossibility.　The animal is certainly rare, as is also a Queen Anne's farthing ; but it is not such a rarity as we are led to believe. On the contrary, specimens are frequently offered for sale at the Zoological Gardens.

It is another great mistake to think that Cats have fleas : the insect infesting a half-grown Cat does not leap like a flea.

The she Cat goes with young from fifty-five to fifty-eight days, and generally has four or five kittens at a litter. When born, they are blind and deaf, like puppies. They get their sight in about nine days, and are about eighteen months before reaching full growth.

Those who wish their Cats to catch mice, I should advise not to neglect the Cat's food. A starved Cat makes a very bad mouser; being too eager and hungry for the work, it tries to pounce upon its prey before the proper time comes. A good mouser does not eat the mouse. I have a black Cat, which is very fat, but a wonderful huntsman, and surprisingly nimble at the chase. He is also as proud of his achievements as a human sportsman, and brings me every head of game he catches. Sometimes, if I have been out when he has caught his mouse, he has gone all over the house in search of me, and at last has taken his seat by the fireside, or out in the garden, and nursed the trophy of his prowess until I returned, mewing piteously if anyone attempted to take it away; but once having laid it at my feet, and had his head scratched in return, his interest in the matter seemed to cease, and he went away without again attempting to touch it. It was clear that he had made me a present of the game; and, as we sometimes think, when we make anyone a present of something to eat, it would be more delicate for us to go away immediately, lest it might be supposed we desired to be asked to stop and partake of it, Tom thus departed, no doubt with a similar idea.

" No experiment," says an intelligent writer, " can be more beautiful than that of setting a kitten for the first time before a looking-glass. The animal appears surprised and pleased with the reflection, and makes several attempts to touch its new acquaintance ; and at length, finding its efforts fruitless, it looks behind the glass, and appears highly astonished at the absence of the figure. It again views itself, and tries to touch the image with its foot, suddenly looking at intervals behind the glass. It then becomes more accurate in its observations, and begins, as it were, to make experiments by stretching out its paw in different directions ; and when it finds that these motions are answered in every respect by the figure in the glass, it seems at length to be convinced of the real nature of the image."

CHAPTER V.

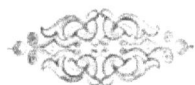

CHAPTER V.

—o—

Of Whittington's Cat, and another Cat that visited Strange Countries.

—o—

S no work about Cats could be complete without the story of Dick Whittington, from the first moment I had made up my mind to write this book, I had also made up my mind to look up the best authorities upon the subject—to write Whittington's Cat's life, and to give her a chapter all to herself. Having come to this conclusion, the question naturally arose where were the authorities. I made search, I read deeply, but I gathered small matter on which I could place reliance, and I was half inclined to abandon my resolve, when happening to have ten minutes to spend, waiting for an omnibus at a street corner in the east-end of London, I made a discovery in a shop window, by the result of which I intend that you shall benefit almost as much as I have myself ; for this discovery was nothing less than the very identical tale-book that I bought when I was a child, only it was a penny now, instead of twopence, as in the days of my extreme youth,—yes, the very identical tale of Whittington and his Cat, with a splendid illustrated pink wrapper and seven magnificent engravings, hand-coloured blue, red, yellow and pink on each plate, with here and there a dash of green laid boldly on, irrespective of outline, and now and again reaching as far as the type. Here, in the well-remembered verses, was Richard's history related :—

" Dick Whittington had often heard
　　The curious story told
　　That far fam'd London's brilliant streets
　　Were paved with sheets of gold ;
　　Sometimes by waggon, erst on foot,
　　Poor Dick he came to town,
　　But found the streets, instead of gold,
　　Were muddy, thick, and brown."

(You will observe that the poet sacrifices every-thing for the rhyme, and I do not blame him, when I contemplate the noble result) :—

> " In search of work he wandered round,
> Till his heart was sick and sore ;
> Then cold and hungry laid him down
> Besides a Merchant's door.
> The Merchant kindly took him in,
> And gave him food to eat,
> But the plainest of plain cooks "—

(Do you notice the poet's wit and humour ?)

> " Him cruelly did treat."

(There is a picture here of the Cook beating Whittington with two ladles.)

> " No longer could he stay,
> So towards the famous Highgate Hill
> Poor Dick he ran away.
> Four miles he ran, then wearied much,
> He sat him on a stone,
> And heard the merry bells of Bow
> Speak to him in this tone—
> ' Turn again, Whittington,
> Thrice Lord Mayor of London.' "

The poet's lines at this point have been beauti-fully illustrated by a picture of Whittington, sitting on the stone aforesaid, labelled " four miles to London," in an attitude of attention, whilst the

G

merry church of Bow is to be seen on the other
side of a wooden fence, apparently fifty yards
off.

> " Then taking heart, he wandered home,
>   But meeting on the road
>   A boy, who had a Cat to sell,
>   He took't to his abode."

(I think, now, that " took't " shows real genius !
How else could you have got over the difficulty ?)

> " She drove away the rats and mice—
>   She was his only friend,"—

(This is true pathos.)

> " But when the Merchant went abroad,
>   He Puss did with him send."

(This part wants thinking over. It means Whittington sent the Cat with his master; please, however, read on) :—

> " It was the only thing he had—
>   Each servant something sent ;
>   The cook became more cruel still
>   After her master went.
>   Meanwhile Puss sail'd across the seas,
>   Unto the Moorish Court,
>   And to the palace of the King
>   The merchant Pussy brought ;

For that poor King no rest enjoy'd
All through the rats and mice,
They swept the food from off his board—
Puss killed them in a trice."

(And I should rather think she did, too, if the artist may be believed who depicts her simultaneously seizing one rat with her teeth, and two others with each of her fore paws.)

" The King then gave him heaps of gold
For an animal so rare ;
The merchant brought it all to Dick,
Oh, how the boy did stare !

(And he is represented staring tremendously at a box, apparently four feet by two-and-a-half, and two-and-a-quarter high, marked " R. W.," and chock full of guineas.)

" The kindly bells had told him true
In saying, ' Turn again,'
For Whittington was thrice Lord Mayor
In great King Henry's reign."

The poem here concludes with a beautiful picture of a gentleman and a lady sitting on chairs of state. I am not quite certain whether this is intended to represent King Henry and his Queen, or Lord and Lady Whittington ; as far as the portrait

goes, I should say that the gentleman was Charles
the First.

In 1857 an advertisement appeared in several
newspapers of a person who was willing to buy any
number of live Cats for exportation. They were
probably wanted for New Zealand; but it is not
every emigrating Puss that is as lucky as Dick
Whittington's (which, of course, by the way, never
existed at all.) As a contrast to the successful
career of the Cat described above, let me tell you,
in almost the same words in which it is amusingly
told in a magazine article, the story of a Cat who
went "some strange countries for to see."

During the bold campaign of Mr. Williams the
Missionary in Polynesia, a favourite Cat was taken
on shore by one of the teacher's wives at their first
visit to the island of Rarotonga. But Tom, not
liking the aspect of his new acquaintance, fled to
the mountains. Under the influence of the apostles
of the new religion, a priest named Tiaki had destroyed his idol. His house was situated at a distance from the settlement, and at midnight, while
he was lying asleep on his mat, his wife, who was
sitting awake by his side, musing upon the strange
events of the day, beheld, with consternation, two
fires glittering in the doorway, and heard with sur-

prise a mysterious and plaintive voice. Petrified with fear, she awoke her husband, and began to up-braid him with his folly for burning his god, who, she declared, was now come to be avenged of them. " Get up and pray !" she cried. The husband arose, and, on opening his eyes, beheld the same glaring lights, and heard the same ominous sound. He commenced with all possible vehemence to vocife-rate the alphabet, as a prayer to the powers above to deliver them from the vengeance of Satan. The Cat, on hearing the incantation, was as much alarmed as the priest and his wife ; so he escaped once more into the wilderness, leaving the repentant priestly pair in ecstacies at the efficacy of their exorcism. The nocturnal apparition of a Cat in the flesh had nearly reinstated an overthrown idol. Subsequently, Puss, in his perambulations, perhaps in hopes of finding a native fur-clad helpmate, went to another distant district ; and as a maral or temple stood in a retired spot, and was shaded by the rich foliage of ancient trees, Tommy, pleased with the situation, and wishing to frequent good society, took up his abode with the wooden gods. A few days after, the priest came, accompanied by a number of worshippers, to present some offering to the pretended deities ; and, on opening the door,

Tom greeted them with a respectful mew. Unaccustomed to such salutations, the priest, instead of returning the welcome with a reciprocal politeness, rushed out of the sanctuary, shouting to his companions, "Here's a monster from the deep! a monster from the deep!"

The whole party of devotees hastened home, collected several hundreds of their brethren, put on their war-caps, brought their spears, clubs, and slings, blackened themselves with charcoal, and, thus equipped, came shouting on to attack the enemy. Tom, affrighted at the formidable array, sprang towards the open door, and, darting through the terror-stricken warriors, sent them scampering in all directions. In the evening, while the brave conspirators were entertaining themselves and a numerous company with a war-dance, to recruit their spirits, poor Tom, wishing to see the sport, and bearing no malice in his heart, stole in amongst them to take a peep. Again the dusky heroes seized their weapons and gave chase to the unfortunate Cat; but "the monster of the deep" was too nimble for them. Some hours afterwards, when all was quiet, Tom unwisely endeavoured to renew his domiciliary relations with man. In the dead of the night he entered a house, crept beneath a coverlet, under which a whole native family were lying, and fell asleep. His purring awoke the man, in the hospitality of whose night-cloth he had taken refuge, and who, supposing that some other monster had come to disturb his household, closed the doorways, awoke the inmates, and procured lights to search for the intruder. Poor Tom, fatigued with the two previous engagements of the day, lay quietly asleep, when the warriors, attacking him with their clubs and spears, thought themselves models of bravery in putting an end to him.

But Cats, though thus misunderstood at first, seem in the end to have proved a welcome and valuable introduction to the country. One of Mr. Williams's means of proselytism was, the exercise of a useful handicraft—he turned blacksmith ; but he found unusual difficulties in the way of his working a forge. Rarotonga was devastated by a plague of rats, which congregated at night in his blacksmith's shop, and devoured every particle of leather, so that, in the morning, nothing remained of his bellows but the bare boards. The rats, however, were not permitted to have everything their own way. The missionaries imported a singular cargo, consisting of pigs, cocoa-nuts, and Cats. The Cats proved a real blessing to the island, but even they did not destroy so many rats as the pigs, which were exceedingly voracious, and took greedily to the rodent diet.

By the way, I must not close the chapter without one little scrap.

Mr. Spectator, in No. 5, March 6, 1711, says :—
"I am credibly informed that there was once a design of casting into an opera the story of Whittington and his Cat, and that in order to do it there had been got together a great quantity of mice, but Mr. Rich, the proprietor of the playhouse, very prudently considered that it would be impossible for the Cat to kill them all."

CHAPTER VI.

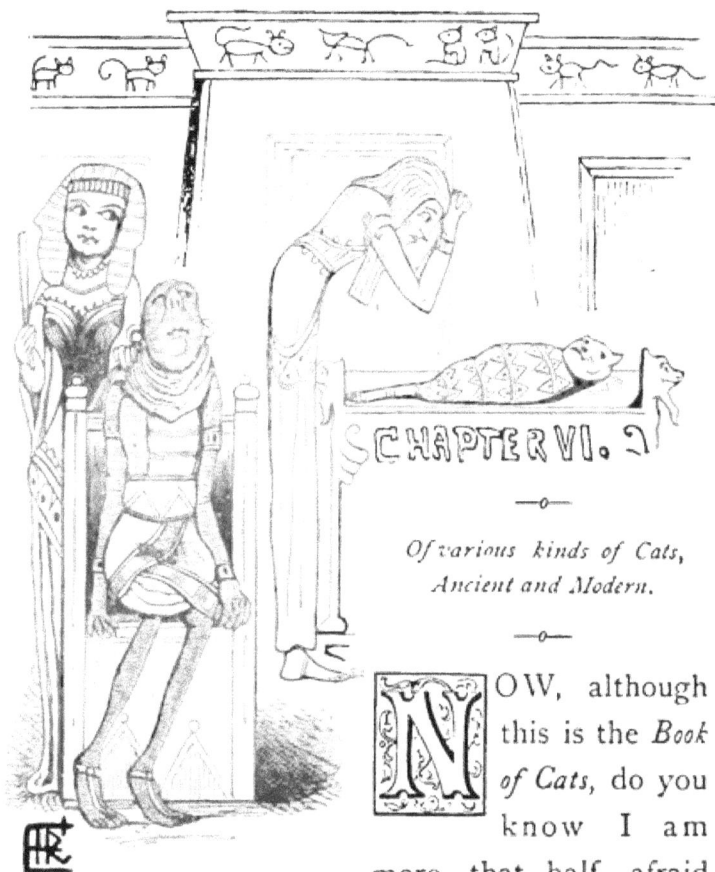

CHAPTER VI.

—o—

Of various kinds of Cats,
Ancient and Modern.

—o—

OW, although this is the *Book of Cats*, do you know I am more that half afraid that if I give you too much about Cats in it, you will go away dissatisfied. Some years ago there was a great rage for mechanics' institutions and instructive lectures on things generally, and one half the world was for jumping on to the platform and improving the mind of the other half in gases and ologies ; and, in those days, there was one particular sort of lecture, which might be roughly described as hard words and an explosion, with which the frequenter of all institutes was perfectly familiar ; and you may remember, too, how we did not so much care about the words, but thought that the stuff out of the bottle, that went off with a bang, was the best fun out. Carried away by the popularity of these oratorical and chemical displays, the heads of schools were wont to encourage lecturing on a small scale among their pupils, only suppressing the explosive part of the entertainment as too dangerous ; and young gentlemen told other young gentlemen what they knew rather better than the young gentlemen telling them respecting the ology of which they treated.

In like fashion, I am afraid I may be only telling you what you know already, or what you might have known, but have not cared about learning. The fact is, all that this chapter contains is to be elsewhere found at greater length. I have no new theories of my own upon the subject, and, indeed, would not presume to argue the question of the domestic Cat's origin with those who have so ably treated the subject in books long since written. To tell the truth, I was not myself very much interested about the matter when I began to read the arguments on either side. Will you be ? I am inclined to think not. However, here is a brief statement of the case, which is easily skipped if not approved of.

M. Rüppel, who discovered in the wild regions west of the Nile a Cat about one-third smaller than the European Cat, and having a longer tail, is of opinion that the animal was descended from the domestic Cat of the ancient Egyptians, and that the Egyptian and our domestic Cat are identical. Temminck is of the same opinion ; but Professor Owen objects to this theory, because the first deciduous molar-tooth of the Egyptian Cat has a relatively thicker crown, and is supported by three roots, whilst the corresponding tooth of the domestic and wild Cat of Europe has a thinner crown, and only two roots. A writer on the subject, in 1836, says, there is no doubt but that the wild Cat of the European forests is the tame Cat of European houses ; that the wild Cat at some period has been domesticated, and that the tame Cat would become wild if turned into the woods. Mr. Bell, however, with regard to the belief that the common wild Cat is the father of the tame, says, that the general conformation of the two animals is con-

siderably different, especially in the length and
form of the tail. The fur, too, of the wild Cat is
thicker and longer.

Sir William Jardine thinks that, since the introduction of our house Cat to this country, there may
have been an accidental cross with the wild native
species, by which the difference in form between
the wild and tame Cat may be accounted for.
" The domestic Cat," says he, " is the only one of
this race which has been generally used in the
economy of man. Some of the other small species
have shown that they might be applied to similar
purposes ; and we have seen that the general disposition of this family will not prevent their training. Much pains would have been necessary to
effect this, and none of the European nations were
likely to have attempted it. The scarcity of Cats
in Europe, in its earliest ages, is also well known,
and in the tenth and eleventh centuries a good
mouser brought a high price."

Another author, quoting the above, says :—

"Although our opinion coincides with that of
Rüppel, and we think that we are indebted to the
superstition of the ancient Egyptians for having
domesticated the species mentioned by Rüppel, we
have no doubt that since its introduction to this

country, and more particularly to the north of
Scotland, there have been occasional crosses with
our native species, and that the result of these
crosses have been kept in our houses. We have
seen many Cats very closely resembling the wild
Cat, and one or two which could scarcely be distinguished from it. There is, perhaps, no other
animal that so soon loses its cultivation and returns apparently to a state completely wild : the
tasting of some wild and living food may tempt
them to seek it again and to leave their civilized
homes. They then prowl about in the same
manner as their prey, couching in the long grass
and brush-wood, and hiding themselves from all
publicity."

No game destroyer, however, is more easily
caught than the Cat. In summer, when rabbit-
paunches will not keep on account of the weather,
a little valerian root is used as a bait. The Cats
come to rub themselves on it, finding some unaccountable pleasure in so doing. The valerian root
is of a whitish colour, and it has a very strong and
disagreeable smell : it is used by us as a medicine
in nervous disorders, and its good effects against
headaches, low-spirits, and trembling of the limbs
are well known. A story is told of a little boy

home for the holidays who played an old lady this trick :—He put some valerian root under the hearth-rug, which set the Cat scratching, rubbing her back on it, and performing a hundred antics, till the old lady, getting frightened, thought Puss had gone mad. The boy then quietly took away the valerian. The Cat grew calm again, and the old lady was much astonished.

It is a cruel custom in some parts of the country to cut off the ears of Cats and remove the hairs all round the exposed aperture of the ear, to prevent the animal from poaching in the woods. It is thought that by so doing, the wet off the bushes and grass may get into the internal cavity of the ear, and by the pain cause the Cat to desist from the chase. Cats so mutilated, however, often choose fine days for their poaching expeditions.

A Cat caught in a trap is a dangerous customer to let loose again. If the door be opened incautiously, the Cat will probably fly at the catcher's face the moment she sees the light. The only safe way of getting the Cat out of the trap is to place a sack over the door end of the trap, and then rattle the other end with a stick. The animal runs at once into the sack.

Wild Cats not only eat birds, but seek eagerly

after their eggs, of which they are passionately fond.

Regarding the wild Cat, Pennant says, " It may be called the ' British Tiger ': it is the fiercest and most destructive beast we have ; making dreadful havoc amongst our poultry, lambs and birds. It inhabits the most mountainous and wooded parts of these islands, living mostly in trees and feeding only at night. It multiplies as fast as our common Cats."

A wild Cat is said to have been killed in Cumberland (my authority gives no date) which measured above five feet in length from the nose to the end of the tail.

Mr. Timbs relates how, in 1850, he saw, at No. 175, Oxford Street, a beautifully-marked tabby Cat weighing 25¾ lbs., and measuring 27 inches round the body, and 37 inches from the tip of the tail to the end of the nose ; height to top of shoulders 11½ inches : he was then seven years old.

The tame Cat's tail ends in a point; the wild Cat's in a tuft. The head of the wild Cat is triangular and strongly marked, the ears triangular, large, long and pointed.

At the village of Barnborough, in Yorkshire,

there is a tradition extant of a serious conflict that once took place between a man and a wild Cat. The inhabitants say that the fight began in an adjacent wood, and that the man and Cat fought from thence to the porch of the church, where each died of the wounds received. A rude painting in the church commemorates the sanguinary event, and the red colour of some of the stones are, of course, said to be blood-stains, which all the soap and water in the world could not remove.

In the reign of Richard II. wild Cats were reckoned among the beasts of the chase, and there was an edict that no man should use more costly apparel than that made of lambs' or Cats'-skins.

In Egypt Cats were considered sacred to the Goddess Bubastis, the Egyptian Diana. Her priestesses were vowed to celibacy: they passed a great portion of their time attending on the Cats of the temple. Mrs. Loudon suggests that hence, perhaps, may have arisen the idea that a fondness for Cats is a sign of old maidism.

Apollo created the lion to terrify his sister Diana, and she turned his fearful beast into ridicule by mimicking it in the form of a Cat. Cats were dedicated to Diana, not only when she bore her proper name, but when she was called "Hecate." Witches who worshipped Hecate had always a favourite Cat.

A very great number of Cats' mummies, discovered in Egypt, afford ample proof of the esteem in which Pussy was held in "Thebes' Streets Three Thousand Years Ago." If one died a natural death, it was mourned for with many ceremonies; among others the entire household, where the death took place, shaved off their eyebrows. If killed, the murderer was given up to the mob to buffet him to death. Cats were held sacred when alive, and when they died were embalmed and deposited in the niches of the catacombs. An insult offered by a Roman to a Cat caused an insurrection among the Egyptians when nothing else could excite them. Cambyses gained Pelusis, which had previously successfully resisted all attacks, by the following stratagem :—He gave to each of his soldiers employed in the attack a live Cat, instead of a buckler, and the Egyptians, rather than hurt the objects of their veneration, suffered themselves to be vanquished without striking a blow.

Herodotus tells us that "on every occasion of a fire in Egypt, the strangest prodigy occurs with the Cats. The inhabitants allow the fire to rage as long as it pleases, while they stand about, at intervals, and watch these animals, which, slipping by the men, or else leaping over them, rush headlong into the flames."

In some of the curious Egyptian pictures at the British Museum, you may see the representation of Cats being trained to catch birds.

Cats are frequently trained in California to catch a species of burrowing pouched rat, called a gopher, a destructive animal infesting fields and gardens. Cats, so trained, are very valuable.

We are are told that there was once a Cape in the Island of Cyprus, which was called Cat Cape. A monastery stood here, the monks of which were compelled by their vows to keep a great number of Cats, to wage war against the snakes, with which the Island was swarming. At the sound of a certain bell the Cats came trooping home to their meals, and then rushed out again to the chase. When, however, the Turks conquered the Island, they destroyed both the Cats and their home.

In the middle ages, animals formed as prominent a part in the worship of the time as in the old religion of Egypt. The Cat was a very important personage in religious festivals. At Aix, in Provence, on the festival of Corpus Christi, the finest Tom-cat of the country, wrapt in swaddling clothes like a child, was exhibited in a magnificent shrine to public admiration. Every knee was bent, every hand strewed flowers, or poured incense, and Grimalkin was treated in all respects as the god of the day. But on the festival of St. John, poor Tom's fate was reversed. A number of the tabby tribe were put into a wicker basket, and thrown alive into the midst of an immense fire, kindled in the public square by the bishop and his clergy. Hymns and anthems were sung, and processions were made by the priest and people in honour of the sacrifice.

In the reign of Howel the Good, who died in 948, a law was made in Wales, fixing the price of the Cat, which was then of great scarcity. A kitten before it got its sight was to cost one penny; until a warranty was given of its having caught a mouse, twopence; after this important event, four-pence, and a very high price, too, the times con-sidered. The Cat, however, was required to be perfect in its senses of seeing and hearing, should be a good mouser, have its claws uninjured, and, if a lady pussy, be a good mamma. If after it was sold, it was found wanting in any of these particu-lars, the seller was to forfeit a third of the purchase-money. If any one stole or killed the Cat that

was guarding the prince's granary, the criminal for-
feited a milch ewe with her fleece and lamb, or as
much wheat as when poured upon a Cat suspended
by its tail, would bury the animal up to the top of
its tail.

In Abyssinia, Cats are so valuable, that a
marriageable girl who is likely to come in for a
Cat, is looked upon as quite an heiress.

The resemblance between the Tiger and the Cat
is so striking, that little children first taken to the
Zoological Gardens almost always call the Tigers
great Cats ; and, in their native woods, Tigers
purr.

The domestic species require no description, but
one or two of the varieties may be mentioned :

The Cat of Angora, is a very beautiful variety,
with silvery hair of fine silken texture, generally
longest on the neck, but also long on the tail. Some
are yellowish, and others olive, approaching to the
colour of the Lion ; but they are all delicate
creatures, and of gentle dispositions. Mr. Wood,
while staying in Paris, made the acquaintance of an
Angora, which ate two plates of almond biscuits at
a sitting. This breed of Cats has singular tastes ;
I knew one that took very kindly to gin and water,
and was rather partial to curry. He also ate peas,

greens, and broad beans (in moderation). Most Cats are fond of asparagus.

The Persian Cat is a variety with hair very long, and very silky, perhaps more so than the Cat of Angora ; it is however differently coloured, being of a fine uniform grey on the upper part, with the texture of the fur as soft as silk, and the lustre glossy; the colour fades off on the lower parts of the sides, and passes into white, or nearly so, on the belly. This is, probably, one of the most beautiful varieties, and it is said to be exceedingly gentle in its manners.

The Chinese Cat has the fur beautifully glossed, but it is very different from either of those which have been mentioned. It is variegated with black and yellow, and, unlike most of the race, has the ears pendulous. Bosman, writing about the ears, says : " It is worthy of observation, that there is in animals evident signs of ancestry of their slavery. Long ears are produced by time and civilization, and all wild animals have straight round ears."

The Tortoise-shell or Spanish Cat is one of the prettiest varieties of those which have the fur of moderate length, and without any particular silvery gloss. The colours are very pure, black, white, and reddish orange ; and, in this country, at least, males thus marked are said to be rare, though they are quite common in Egypt and the south of Europe. This variety has other qualities to recommend it, besides the beauty of its colours. Tortoise-shell Cats are very elegant, though delicate in their form, and are, at the same time, very active, and among the most attached and grateful of the whole race.

Bluish grey is not a common colour ; this species are styled "Chartreux Cats," and are esteemed rarities.

The Manx Cat is perhaps the most singular ; its limbs are gaunt, its fur close set, its eyes staring and restless, and it has no tail ; that is to say, there is only a sort of knob as though its tail had been amputated.   "A black Manx Cat," says a modern writer, "with its staring eyes and its stump of a tail, is a most measly looking beast, which would find a more appropriate resting place at Kirk Alloway or the Black Bay, than at the fireside of a respectable household. So it might fitly be the quadrupedal form in which the ancient sorcerers were wont to clothe themselves on their nocturnal excursions."

I read in an article by Mr. Lord that there is a variety of tailless Cats found in various parts of the world, and he suggests that this deficiency may be due to an accident originally, but perpetuated by interbreeding. I am not quite of the same opinion. It reminds one of the old saying, "It runs in the blood, like wooden legs."

I recollect the case of a young gentleman who devoted his leisure evenings to cutting off Cats' tails in the neighbourhood in which he lived. He hung them up in bunches to dry, and had rare sport, while it lasted, in making the collection, only some one, who was a Cat-owner, did not see the fun of it, and put an end to the joke. Some young men think it a manly sport to kill or hunt down Cats; and, by the way, do you remember Sir Robert Peel's memorable speech about the Volunteers, thus reported in *Hansard?*—

"At Hythe the first prize was carried off by a genuine Cockney. Upon being asked how he had acquired his extraordinary skill and precision—

"'Oh,' said he, as reported in the columns of the *Court Journal,* 'I live in London, and have had considerable practice in shooting at the Cats of my Brompton neighbours.'

"It was not, perhaps, of much consequence in the depth of winter (continued Sir R. Peel), but no man could tell what a scene London would present in the height of the season. Everybody would be shooting at his neighbour's Cat. There would be the stoker of the Railway Rifles potting at the funnels of the North Western, and we should have the Finsbury Filibusters fluking over Cripplegate. He trusted, however, that before that time a stop would be put to the Volunteer movement," etc., etc.

Cats do certainly seem to enjoy themselves on moonlight nights, anyhow they make noise enough. The Cat was believed by the ancients to stand in some relation to the moon, for Plutarch says that the Cat was the symbol of the moon on account of her different colours, her busy ways at night, and her giving birth to twenty-eight young ones during the course of her life, which is exactly the number of the phases of the moon.

The ancients identified Bubastis with the Greek Artemis (or Diana), and each was regarded as the Goddess of the moon. Bubastis was generally represented as a woman with a Cat's head.

It might occur to some, that " Puss " is derived from the Egyptian name, *Pasht ;* but perhaps it is better to acquiesce in the derivation from the Latin, *Pusus* (a little boy), or *Pusa* (a little girl). By others this term is thought to be a corruption of *Pers.*

The French of Cat is *Chat;* the German, *Katze;* the Italian, *Gatto;* the Spanish, *Gato;* the Dutch and Danish, *Kat;* the Welsh, *Cath;* the Latin, *Catus :* the French of Puss is *Minette.* You have heard the story, I suppose, of the person who being told to decline the noun Cat, when he came to the vocative, said " O Cat !" on which he was reminded that if he spoke to a Cat he would say " Puss."

Mr. Buchton says, that " the only language in which the name of the Cat is significant, is the Zend, where the word *Gatu,* almost identical with the Spanish *Gato,* means a place—a word peculiarly significant in reference to this animal, whose attachment is peculiar to place, and not to the person, so strikingly indicated by the dog."

In some parts of Lancashire, a Tom is still called a " Gib " or "Gibbe" Cat, the *g* being pronounced *hard,* not *jibbe,* as found in most dictionaries. According to Nares, Gib, the contraction of Gilbert, was the name formerly applied to a Cat, as Tom is now, and that Tibert, as given in *Reynard the Fox,* was the old French for Gilbert. Chaucer in his *Romance of the Rose* translates *Thibert le Cas* by " Gibbe our Cat." Shakespeare applies the word Gibbe to an old worn-out animal. The term Gib-face means the lower lip of a horse. In mechanics, the pieces of

iron employed to clasp together the pieces of wood
or metal of a frame which is to be keyed previous
to inserting the keys, are called Gibs.   Anyone
curious upon the subject of Gib Cats, my find the
subject treated at length in the *Etymologicon*.

CHAPTER VII.

—0—

Of some Clever Cats.

—0—

THIS domestic animal, as Dr. Johnson puts it, "that catches mice," can do many other things when it has a fair opportunity of distinguishing itself. It is difficult, but by no means impossible, to teach a Cat tricks. I myself had a favourite Cat, lately dead, which performed a variety of amusing feats, though I must own that it was extremely coquettish, and nine times out of ten refused to exhibit before a visitor, invited specially to witness the little comedy.   Many Cats, without teaching, learn droll tricks.

Doctor Smellie tells of a Cat that had learned to lift the latch of a door; and other tales have been related of Cats that have been taught to ring a bell by hanging to the bell rope; and this anecdote is related by the illustrious Sam Slick, of Slickville.   It occurred, several times, that his servant entered the library without having been summoned by his master, and in all cases the domestic was quite sure he had heard the bell.   Great wonderment was caused by this, and the servant began to suspect that the house was haunted.   It was, at length, noticed that on all these mysterious occasions the Cat entered with the servant.   She was, therefore, watched, and it was soon perceived that whenever she found the library door closed against her, she jumped on to the window-sill, and thence sprang at the bell.   This feat was exhibited to several of the clockmaker's friends, for the Cat when shut out of the room, would at once resort to this mode of obtaining admission.

My third story is a time-honoured one that almost every person who has written about Cats has related.   There was once upon a time, a

THE CUNNING CAT.

monastery, a Cat, and a dinner-bell. Every day at a certain hour the bell was rung, and the monks and the Cat had their meal together. There however came a time when, during the bell ringing, the Cat happened to be locked in a room at the other end of the building. Some hours afterwards she was released, and ran straight to the refectory, to find, alas! nothing but bare tables to welcome her. Presently the monks were astonished by a loud summons from the dinner-bell. Had the cook, in his absence of mind, prepared another dinner? Some of them hurried to the spot, where they found the Cat swinging on the bell-rope. She had learnt from experience that there never was any dinner without a bell ringing; and by force of reasoning, no doubt, had come to the conclusion that the dinner would be sure to come if she only rang loud enough.

But that story is not half so wonderful as another, about an Angora Cat belonging to a Carthusian monastery at Paris. This ingenious animal discovered that, when a certain bell rang, the cook left the kitchen to answer it, leaving the monks' dinners, portioned out in plates, unprotected. The plan the Cat adopted was to ring the bell, the handle of which hung outside the kitchen by the side of a window, to leap through the window, and back

I

again when she had secured one of the portions.
This little manœuvre she carried on for some
weeks before the perpetrator of the robbery was
discovered ; and there is no saying, during this
lapse of time, how many innocent persons were
unjustly suspected.　Who shall say, indeed, but
that the head of the establishment did not, as in
the great Jackdaw case, call for his candle, his bell,
and his book, and in holy anger, in pious grief,
solemnly curse that rascally thief, as, you remember, the Cardinal cursed the Jackdaw :—

> " He cursed him at board, he cursed him in bed,
>   From the sole of his foot to the crown of his head ;
>   He cursed him in eating, he cursed him in drinking,
>   He cursed him in coughing, in sneezing, in winking ;
>   He cursed him in sitting, in standing, in lying ;
>   He cursed him in walking, in riding, in flying ;
>   He cursed him in living, he cursed him in dying ;—
>   Never was heard such a terrible curse !
>   But what gave rise
>   To no little surprise,
>   Nobody seemed one penny the worse !"

When, however, they found out that Pussy was
the wrong-doer, and, unlike the Jackdaw, had grown
fat upon her misdeeds, they did not hang her, as
you might suppose, though I have no doubt that
course was suggested ; on the contrary, they allowed

her to pursue her nefarious career, and charged
visitors a small fee to be allowed to see her do it.
Out of evil sometimes may come good; but one
would hardly think that the best way of making a
person's fortune was to rob him.

Cats have been frequently known to do their
best to protect the property of their masters, as
well as dogs. A man who was imprisoned for a
burglary, in America, stated after his conviction,
that he, and two others broke into the house of a
gentleman, near Harlem. While they were in the
act of plundering it, a large black Cat flew at one
of the robbers, and fixed her claws on each side of
his face. He added, that he never saw a man so
frightened in his life; and that in his alarm, he
made such an outcry, that they had to beat a
precipitate retreat, to avoid detection.

A lady in Liverpool had a favourite Cat. She
never returned home, after a short absence, without
being joyfully received by it. One Sunday, however, on returning from church, she was surprised to
find that Pussy did not receive her as usual, and its
continued absence made her a little uneasy. The
servants were all appealed to, but none could
account for the circumstance. The lady, therefore,
made a strict search for her feline friend, and

descending to the lower storey, was surprised to hear her cries of " Puss " answered by the mewing of a Cat, the sounds proceeding from the wine cellar, which had been properly locked and the key placed in safe custody. As the Cat was in the parlour when the lady left for church, it was unnecessary to consult a " wise man " to ascertain that the servants had clandestine means of getting into the wine-cellar, and that they had forgotten, when they them-selves returned, to request pussy, also, to withdraw. The contents of the cellar, from that time forward, did not disappear as quickly as they had been doing for some time previously.

A woman was murdered at Lyons, and when the body was found weltering in blood, a large white Cat was seen mounted on the cornice of a cup-board. He sat motionless, his eyes fixed on the corpse, and his attitude and looks expressing horror and affright. Next morning he was still found there ; and when the room was filled by the officers of justice, neither the clattering of the soldiers' arms nor the loud conversation frightened him away. As soon, however, as the suspected persons were brought in, his eyes glared with fury, and his hair bristled. He darted into the middle of the room, where he stopped for a moment to gaze on them, and then fled precipitately. The faces of the assassins showed, for the first time, signs of guilt: they were afterwards brought to trial, condemned, and, before execution, confessed.

In September, 1850, the mistress of a public house in the Commercial Road, London, going late at night into the tap-room, found her Cat in a state of great excitement. It would not suffer itself to be stroked, but ran wildly, to and fro, between its mistress and the chimney-piece, mewing loudly. The landlady alarmed, summoned assistance, and presently a robber was discovered up the chimney. Upon his trial it was proved that he had robbed several public-houses, by remaining last in the tap-room, and concealing himself in a similar manner.

An old maiden lady, rich and miserly, had, in the latter years of her life, placed all her affections upon a Cat she called " Minny," for which she had made a fine bed-place in the wainscot, over a closet in the parlour, where she kept the animal's provisions. The food in question was stowed away in a drawer, and under the drawer which served as Minny's safe, was another, very artfully concealed, and closing with a spring. To the latter the Cat had often seen its mistress pay lengthened visits. When the old lady died, her heirs came to live in

the house, and Minny being no longer fed with the
same regularity, was often hungry, and would then
go and scratch at the drawer where its food had
been kept.   The drawer being at length opened,
some pieces of meat were found within in a mum-
mified state.   These having been given to the Cat,
failed to console her, and she scratched harder than
ever at the secret drawer underneath ; and Minny's
new masters, in course of time understanding what
she meant, broke it open, and found twenty small
canvas bags of guineas snugly packed up within.
My authority does not say how Minny fared after
this little discovery.   Let us hope she was allowed
her old sleeping-place, and got her food with toler-
able regularity.   But there is no knowing.

Cats are very fond of creeping into out-of-the-
way holes and corners, and, sometimes, pay dearly
for so doing.

Once when repairing the organ in Westminster
Abbey, a dried Cat was found in one of the large
recumbent wooden pipes, which had been out of
tune for some time.   In one of the rooms at the
Foreign Office, some years ago, there was, for a
long time, a very disagreeable smell, which was supposed to arise from the drains.   At length some
heavy volumes being taken down from a shelf, the

body of a dried Cat was found behind them. The
unfortunate animal had been shut up by accident,
and starved to death, a prisoner, like the heroine
of the " Oak Chest."

Mrs. Loudon, in her book of *Domestic Pets*, tells
several amusing stories. Her mother, the writer
says, had a servant who disliked Cats very much,
and in particular a large black Cat, which she was
in the habit of beating, whenever she could do so
unobserved. The Cat disliked and feared the girl
exceedingly ; however, one day, when her enemy
was carrying some dishes down-stairs into the
kitchen, and had both her hands full, the Cat flew
at her and scratched her hands and face severely.

A strange Cat had two kittens in a stable belonging to the house, and one day, pitying its wretched
condition, Mrs. Loudon ordered her some milk.
A large Tom Cat, attached to the establishment,
watched the proceeding very attentively, and while
the Cat was lapping, went to the stable, brought
out one of the kittens in his mouth, and placed it
beside the saucer, and then fetched the other, looking up into the lady's face, and mewing when he
had done so, as much as to say, " You have fed the
mother, so you may as well feed the children,"
which was done ; and it should be added, for the

credit of Tom's character, that he never attempted
to touch the milk himself.

But the best story is this :—Mrs. Loudon had a
Cat which had unfortunately hurt its leg.   During
the whole time the leg was bad, that lady constantly
gave it milk ; but, at last, she found out that, though
the Cat had become quite well, yet whenever it
saw her, it used to walk lame and hold up its paw,
as though it were painful to put it to the ground.

A favourite Cat, much petted by her mistress,
was one day struck by a servant.   She resented the
injury so much that she refused to eat anything
which he gave her.   Day after day he handed her
dinner to her, but she sat in sulky indignation,
though she eagerly ate the food as soon as it was
offered to her by any other person.   Her resent-
ment continued, undiminished, for upwards of six
weeks.

The same Cat, having been offended by the
housemaid, watched three days before she found a
favourable opportunity for retaliation.   The housemaid was on her knees, washing the passage, when
the Cat went up to her and scratched her arm, to
show her that no one should illuse her with im-
punity.   It is, however, but fair to record her good
qualities as well as her bad ones.   If her resent-

ment was strong, her attachment was equally so, and she took a singular mode of showing it. All the tit-bits she could steal from the pantry, and all the dainty mice she could catch, she invariably brought and laid at her mistress's feet. She has been known to bring a mouse to her door in the middle of the night, and mew till it was opened, when she would present it to her mistress. After doing this she was quiet and contented.

Just before the earthquake at Messina, a merchant of that town noticed that his Cats were scratching at the door of his room, in a state of great excitement. He opened the door for them, and they flew down-stairs and began to scratch more violently still at the street-door. Filled with wonder, the master let them out and followed them through the town out of the gates, and into the fields beyond, but, even then, they seemed half mad with fright, and scratched and tore at the grass. Very shortly the first shock of the earthquake was felt, and many houses (the merchant's among them) came thundering in ruins to the ground.

A family in Callander had in their possession a favourite Tom Cat, which had, upon several occasions, exhibited more than ordinary sagacity. One day, Tom made off with a piece of beef, and the servant followed him cautiously, with the intention of catching, and administering to him a little wholesome correction. To her amazement, she saw the Cat go to a corner of the yard where she knew a rat-hole existed, and lay the beef down by the side of it. Leaving the beef there, he hid himself a short distance off, and watched until a rat made its appearance. Tom's tail then began to wag, and just as the rat was moving away with the bait, he sprang upon, and killed it.

It one day occurred to M. de la Croix that he ought to try an experiment upon a Cat with an air pump. The necessity for her torture was not, however, so apparent to the intended victim of science as to the scientific experimenter. Therefore, when she found the air growing scarce, and discovered how it was being exhausted, she stopped up the valve with her paw. Then M. de la Croix let the air run back, and Pussy took away her paw, but as soon as he began to pump, she again stopped up the hole. This baffled the man of science, and there is no knowing what valuable discovery might have been made, had not his feline friend been so very unaccommodating.

Dr. Careri, in his *Voyage round the World* in 1695, says, that a person, in order to punish a mischievous monkey, placed upon the fire a cocoa nut, and then hid himself, to see how the monkey would take it from the fire without burning his paws. The cunning creature looked about, and seeing a Cat by the fireside, held her head in his mouth, and with her paws took off the nut, which he then threw into water to cool, and ate it.

Cats have always been famous for the wonderful manner in which they have found their way back to their old home, when they have been taken from it, and for this reason alone, have often been accused of loving only the house and not its inmates. It is more probable though, I should think, that the animal returns to the place because its associations there have been happy, and, in the confusion and strangeness of the new house, it cannot comprehend that its old friends have come with it. For instance, I have known a Cat when taken away from a house, return to it, and going from room to room, mew pitifully, in search of the former inmates. When taken away a second time, the new place having in the meantime been set straight, it found nothing to frighten it there, and returned no more to its old house.

I knew a person who was in the habit of moving about a great deal, and hiring furnished houses, who

had a Cat called Sandy, on account of his colour,
which he found in the first instance, in a sort of half-
wild state, on Hampstead Heath, mostly living up a
tree. It had been left behind by the people who had
last occupied the house, and locked out by the landlady. It was about nine or ten years old, and good-
ness knows how many dwelling places it may have
had; with its new friends, I know of five or six
changes, and am told that it always made itself perfectly at home in half an hour after entering a new
house. It was taken from place to place in a
hamper, and the lid being raised would put out
its head and sniff the air in the drollest manner.
Getting out very cautiously, it would then make a
tour of the premises, and inspect the furniture ; at
the end of about half an hour it washed its face
and seemed settled.

A lady residing in Glasgow had a handsome
Cat sent to her from Edinburgh : it was conveyed
to her in a close basket in a carriage. The animal
was carefully watched for two months ; but having
produced a pair of young ones at the end of that
time, she was left to her own discretion, which she
very soon employed in disappearing with both her
kittens. The lady at Glasgow wrote to her friend
at Edinburgh, deploring her loss, and the Cat was

supposed to have formed some new attachment. About a fortnight, however, after her disappearance from Glasgow, her well-known mew was heard at the street-door of her Edinburgh mistress; and there she was with both her kittens, they in the best state, but she, herself, very thin. It is clear that she could carry only one kitten at a time. The distance from Glasgow to Edinburgh is forty-four miles, so that if she brought one kitten part of the way, and then went back for the other, and thus conveyed them alternately, she must have travelled 120 miles at least. She, also, must have journeyed only during the night, and must have resorted to many other precautions for the safety of her young.

Mr. Lord relates a story of a Cat living with some friends of his in a house on an island. The family changed residence, and the Cat was sewn up in a hamper and taken round to the other side of the island in a boat. The island was sparsely inhabited, timbered, and there were but few paths cut to traverse it by, and yet the Cat found its way during the night back again to its old residence. There could have been no scent of foot-prints, neither was there any road or path to guide it.

Another Cat was conveyed from its home in Jamaica to a place five miles distant, and during the time of its transport was sown up closely in a bag. Between the two places were two rivers, one of them about eighty feet broad, deep, and running strong; the other wider and more rapid. The Cat must have swum these rivers, as there were no bridges; but in spite of all obstacles, she made her way back to the house from which she had been taken.

In 1819 a favourite Tabby belonging to a ship-master was left on shore, by accident, while his vessel sailed from the harbour of Aberdour, Fife-shire, which is about half a mile from the village. The vessel was a month absent, and on her return, to the astonishment of the shipmaster, Puss came on board with a fine stout kitten in her mouth, ap-parently about three weeks old, and went directly down into the cabin. Two others of her young ones were afterwards caught, quite wild, in a neigh-bouring wood, where she must have remained with them until the return of the ship. The shipmaster did not allow her, again, to go on shore, otherwise it is probable she would have brought all her family on board. It was very remarkable, because vessels were daily going in and out of the harbour, none of which she ever thought of visiting till the one she had left returned.

In a parish in Norfolk, not six miles from the town of Bungay, lived a clergyman, who, having a Cat, sentenced it to transportation for life because it had committed certain depredations on his larder. But the worthy gentleman found it far easier to pronounce the sentence than to carry it into execution. Poor Puss was first taken to Bungay, but had hardly got there when she escaped, and was soon at home again. Her morals, however, had in no way improved, and a felonious abstraction of butcher's meat immediately occurred. This time the master determined to send the hardened culprit away to a distance, which, as he expressed it, "she would not walk in a hurry." He accordingly gave her (generous man) to a person living at Fakenham, distant at least forty miles. The man called for her in the morning, and carried her off in a bag, that she might not know by what road he went. Vain hope! She knew well enough the way home, as he found to his cost, for directly the house-door was opened the next morning, she rushed out and he saw no more of her. The night after a faint mewing was heard outside the minister's dwelling, but not being so rare an occurrence no attention was paid to it. However, on opening the door next morning, there lay the very Cat which he thought was forty miles away, her feet all cut and blistered, from the hardness of the road, and her silky fur all clotted and matted together with dust and dirt. She had her reward; however her thievish propensities might annoy him, the worthy vicar resolved never again to send her away from the house she loved so well, and exerted herself so nobly to regain.

The Rev. Mr. Wood furnishes some curious particulars of two commercial Cats of his acquaintance, which he very comically describes :—

"I will tell you," says he, "something about our Mincing Lane Cats. Their home was in the cellar, and their habits and surroundings, as you may imagine, from the locality, were decidedly commercial. We had one cunning old black fellow, whose wisdom was acquired by sad experience. In early youth, he must have been very careless ; he then was always getting in the way of the men and the wine cases, and frequent were the disasters he suffered through coming into collision with moving bodies. His ribs had often been fractured, and when nature repaired them, she must have handed them over to the care of her 'prentice hand,' for the

work was done in rather a rough and knotty
manner. This battered and suffering Pussy was at
last assisted by a younger hero, which, profiting by
the teachings of his senior, managed to avoid the
scrapes which had tortured the one who was self-
educated. These two Cats, Junior and Senior, appeared to swear (Cats will swear) eternal friendship
at first sight. An interchange of good offices was
at once established. Senior taught Junior to avoid
men's feet and wine cases in motion, and pointed
out the favourite hunting grounds, while Junior
offered to his Mentor the aid of his activity and
physical prowess.

Senior had a cultivated and epicurean taste for
mice, though he was too old to catch them ; he
therefore entered into a solemn league and covenant
with the junior to this effect :—It was agreed between the two contracting powers, that Junior should ·
devote his energies to catching mice for the benefit
of Senior, who, in consideration of such service, was
to relinquish his claim to a certain daily allowance of
Cat's meat in favour of Junior. This courteous com-
pact was actually and seriously carried out. It was
an amusing and touching spectacle, to behold young
Pussy gravely laying at the feet of his elder the
contents of his game bag; on the other hand, Senior,

K

true to his bargain, licking his jaws and watching Junior steadily consuming a double allowance of Cat's meat.

Senior had the rare talent of being able to carry a bottle of champagne from one end of the cellar to the other, perhaps a distance of a hundred and fifty feet. The performance was managed in this wise. You gently and lovingly approached the Cat as if you did not mean to perpetrate anything wicked; having gained his confidence by fondly stroking his back, you suddenly seized his tail, and by that member raised the animal bodily from the ground—his fore feet sprawling in the air ready to catch hold of any object within reach. You then quickly brought the bottle of wine to the seizing point; Pussy clutched the object with a kind of despairing grip. By means of the aforesaid tail, you carefully carried pussy, bottle and all, from one part of the cellar to the other. Pussy, however, soon became disgusted with this manœuvre, and whenever he saw a friend with a bottle of champagne looming, he used to beat a precipitate retreat.

The reverend gentleman before quoted, had at one time in his possession a marvellously clever little Cat, which he called " Pret," and concerning which he relates a host of anecdotes ; from them are culled the following :—

Pret knew but one fear, and had but few hates. The booming sound of thunder smote her with terror, and she most cordially hated grinding organs and singular costumes. At the sound of a thunderclap poor Pret would fly to her mistress for succour, trembling in every limb. If the dreaded sound occurred in the night or early morning, Pret would leap on the bed and crawl under the clothes as far as the very foot. If the thunder came on by day, Pret would climb on her mistress's knees, put her paws round her neck and hide her face between them with deliberation.

She disliked music of all kinds, but bore a special antipathy to barrel organs ; probably because the costume of the organ-grinder was as unpleasing to her eyes, as his doleful sounds were to her ears. But her indignation reached the highest bounds at the sight of a Greenwich pensioner accoutred in those grotesque habiliments with which the crippled defenders of their country are forced to invest their battered frames. It was the first time that so uncouth an apparition had presented itself to her eyes, and her anger seemed only equalled by her astonishment. She got on the window sill, and there chafed and growled with a sound resembling the miniature roar of a lion. When thus excited she used to present a strange appearance, owing to a crest or ridge of hair which then erected itself on her back, and extended from the top of her head to the root of her tail, which latter member was marvellously expanded. Gentle as she was in her ordinary demeanour, Pret was a terrible Cat when she saw cause, and was undaunted by size or numbers.

She had a curious habit of catching mice by the very tips of their tails, and of carrying the poor little animals about the house, dangling miserably from her jaws. Apparently her object in so doing was to present her prey uninjured to her mistress, who she evidently supposed would enjoy a game with a mouse as well as herself, for like human beings she judged the characters of others by her own. This strange custom of tail-bearing was carried into the privacy of her own family, and caused rather ludicrous results. When Pret became a mother, and desired to transport her kittens from one place to another, she followed her acquired habit of porterage, and tried to carry her kittens about by the tips of their tails. As might be supposed, they objected to this mode of conveyance, and sticking their claws in the carpet, held firmly to the ground, mewing piteously, while their mother was tugging at their tails. It was absolutely necessary to release the kittens from their painful position, and to teach Pret how a kitten ought to be carried. After a while, she seemed to comprehend the state of things, and ever afterwards carried her offspring by the nape of the neck. At one time, when she was yet in her kittenhood, another kitten lived in the same house, and very much annoyed Pret, by coming into the room and eating the meat that had been laid out for herself. However, Pret soon got over the difficulty, by going to the plate as soon as it was placed at her accustomed spot, picking out all the large pieces of meat and hiding them under the table. She then sat down quietly, placing herself sentry over her hidden treasure, while the intruding Cat entered the room, walked up to the plate, and finished the little scraps of meat that Pret had thought fit to leave. After the obnoxious individual had left the room, Pret brought her concealed treasures from their hiding-place and consumed them with deliberation.

Clever as Pret was, she sometimes displayed a most unexpected simplicity of character. After the fashion of the Cat tribe, she delighted in covering up the remainder of her food with any substance that seemed most convenient. She was accustomed, after taking her meals, to fetch a piece of paper and lay it over the saucer, or to put her paw in her mistress's pocket and extract her handkerchief for the same purpose. This little performance showed some depth of reasoning in the creature, but she would sometimes act in a manner totally opposed to rational actions. Paper or handkerchief failing, she has been often seen, after partly finishing her meal, to fetch one of her kittens and to lay it over the plate for the purpose of covering up the remaining food. When kitten, paper, and handkerchief were all wanting, she did her best to scratch up the carpet and lay the fragments over the plate. She has been known, in her anxiety to find a covering for the superabundant food, to drag a tablecloth from its proper locality, and to cause a sad demolition of the superincumbent fragile ware. Please to remember that I have the above upon Mr. Wood's authority, not my own.

Regarding the attachment of Cats to places, the following remarks of the late Rev. Cæsar Otway, in his lecture on the Intellectuality of Domestic Animals before the Royal Zoological Society of Ireland, some years ago, deserve attention. "Of Cats," he says, "time does not allow me to say

much, but this I must affirm, that they are mis-
represented, and often the victims of prejudice. It
is strictly maintained that they have little or no
affection for *persons*, and that their partialities are
confined to *places*. I have known many instances
of the reverse. When leaving, about fifteen years
ago, a glebe-house to remove into Dublin, the Cat
that was a favourite with me, and with my children,
was left behind, in our hurry. On seeing strange
faces come into the house, she instantly left it, and
took up her abode in the top of a large cabbage
stalk, whose head had been cut off, but which retained a sufficient number of leaves to protect poor
Puss from the weather. In this position she remained, and nothing could induce her to leave it,
until I sent a special messenger to bring her to my
house in town. At present I have a Cat that
follows my housekeeper up and down like a Dog ;
every morning she comes up at daybreak in winter
to the door of the room in which the maid servants
sleep, and there she mews until they get up."

I think I ought to conclude my chapter of Clever
Cats with this story, which, though old, is funny :—
There was a lady of Potsdam, living with her little
children, one of whom, while at play, ran a splinter

into her foot, causing her to scream violently. The elder sister was asleep at the time, but awakened by the child's cries, and while just in the act of getting up to quiet it, observed a favourite Cat, with whom the children were wont to play, and which was of a remarkably gentle disposition, leave its seat by the fire, go to the crying baby, and give her a smart blow on the cheek with one of her paws ; after which, Puss walked back with the greatest composure and gravity to her place, as if satisfied with her own conduct, and with the hope of being able to go on with her nap undisturbed.

CHAPTER VIII.

CAT AND DOG LIFE.

Page 139.

BEWARE
DOGS

CHAPTER VIII.

—o—

*Of some amiable Cats, and Cats
that have been good Mothers.*

—o—

TO lead a " Cat
and Dog life "
means a good
deal of scratch-
ing and biting; but Dogs
and Cats have been known to get on very amiably
before now.

There was a Cat which had formed a very warm
friendship with a large Newfoundland dog: she
continually caressed him—advanced in all haste
when he came home, with her tail erect, and rubbed

her head against him, purring with delight. When he lay before the kitchen fire, she used him as a bed, pulling up and settling his hair with her claws to make it comfortable. As soon as she had arranged it to her liking, she lay down upon him, and fell asleep. The dog bore this combing of his locks with patient placidity, turning his head towards her during the operation, and sometimes gently licked her.

Pincher and Puss were sworn friends. Puss had a young family, with whom Pincher was on visiting terms. The nursery was at the top of the house. One day there was a storm ; Puss was upstairs with the babies, and Pincher was in the parlour. Pincher evidently was disturbed by the thunder. Presently Puss came down-stairs mewing, went straight to Pincher, rubbed her cheek against his, and touched him gently with her paw, and then walked to the door, and, looking back, mewed, as though asking him go with her. But Pincher was himself sorely afraid, and could render no assistance. Puss grew desperate, and having renewed her application with increased energy, but without success, at last left the room, mewing piteously, while Pincher sat, with a guilty face, evidently knowing his conduct was selfish. A lady, who had watched this scene, went out to look after the Cat, when the animal, mewing, led the way to a bed-room on the first floor, from under a wardrobe in which a small voice was heard crying. Puss had brought one of her babies down-stairs, and was racked with anxiety respecting its welfare while she fetched the others. It was as clear as possible she wanted Pincher to lend a paw —that is to say, look after this isolated infant while she brought down the rest. The lady took up the kitten in her arms, and accompanied Puss up-stairs, then moved the little bed from the window, through which the lightning had been flashing so vividly as to alarm Puss for the safety of her family. She remained with the Cat until the storm had subsided, and all was calm. On the following morning, the lady was much surprised to find Puss waiting for her outside her bed-room door, and she went with her down-stairs to breakfast, sat by her side, and caressed her in every possible way. Puss had always been in the habit of going down with the lady of the house, but on this occa-sion she had resisted all her mistress's coaxing to leave the other lady's door, and would not go away until she made her appearance. She re-mained till breakfast was over, then went up-stairs to her family. She had never done this before,

and never did it again.   She had shown her gratitude for the lady's care of her little ones, and her
duty was done.

A gentleman, residing in Sussex, had a Cat
which showed the greatest attachment for a young
blackbird, which was given to her by a stable-boy
for food a day or two after she had been deprived
of her kittens.   She tended it with the greatest
care ; they became inseparable companions, and
no mother could show a greater fondness for her
offspring than she did for the bird.

This incongruity of attachment in animals will
generally be found to arise either from the feelings
of natural affection which the mother is possessed
of, or else from that love of sociability, and dislike
of being alone, which is possessed, more or less, by
every created being.

A Horse and Cat were great friends, and the
latter generally slept in the manger.   When the
horse was about to be fed, he always took up the
Cat gently by the skin of the neck, and dropped
her into the next stall, that she might not be in his
way while he was feeding.   At other times, he was
pleased to have her near him.

Mr. Bingley tells of a friend of his who had a
Cat and Dog that were always fighting.   At last

the dog conquered, and the Cat was driven away ; but the servant, whose sweetheart the dog disturbed, poisoned him, and his body was carried lifeless into the courtyard. The Cat, from a neighbouring roof, was observed to watch the motions of several persons who went up to look at him, and when all had retired, he descended and crept cautiously towards the body, then patted it with his paw. Apparently satisfied that the dog's day was over, Puss re-entered the house and washed his face before the fire.

The Reverend Gilbert White, in his amusing book, tells of a boy, who having taken three little young squirrels in their nest or "dray," put these small creatures under the care of a Cat that had lately lost her kittens, and found that she nursed and suckled them with the same assiduity and affection as if they were her own offspring. This circumstance, to some extent, corroborates the stories told of deserted children being nurtured by female beasts of prey who had lost their young, of the truth of which some authors have seriously vouched. Many people went to see the little squirrels suckled by the Cat, and the foster mother became jealous of her charge, and fearing for their safety, hid them over the ceiling, where one died. This circumstance proves her affection for the fondlings, and that she supposed them to be her young. In like fashion hens, when they have hatched ducklings, are as attached to them as though they were their own chickens.

The first public exhibition of a "happy family" in England, was one started at Coventry, about thirty-two years ago, and began with Cats, Rats, and Pigeons in one cage. The proprietor of a happy family gave Mr. Henry Mayhew some amusing particulars on the subject. Among other things, he said that Mr. Monkey was very fond of the Cat, probably for warmth. He would cuddle her for an hour at a time, but if Miss Pussy would not lie still to suit his comfort, he would hug her round the neck and try to pull her down. If then she became vexed, he would be afraid to face her, but stealing slily behind, would give her tail end a nip with his teeth. The Cat and Monkey were the best of friends as long as Miss Pussy would lie still to be cuddled, and suit his convenience. The Monkey would be Mr. Master in a happy family. For that reason the proprietor would not allow either of his Cats to kitten in the cage, because Mr. Monkey would be sure to want to know all about it, and then it would be open war, for if he went to touch

Miss Pussy or her babies, there would be a fight.
Now a Monkey is always very fond of anything
young, such as a kitten, and he and Miss Pussy
would want to nurse the children. The Monkey
liked very much to get hold of a kitten and he
would nurse it in his arms like a baby. The Cats
and the Birds were good friends indeed: they would
perch on her back, and even on her head, and peck
at her fur. A strange Cat was introduced into the
cage, and the moment she made her entry, she
looked round in a scared way, and made a dart
upon the animal nearest her, namely the owl; the
Monkey immediately ran behind and bit her tail,
and the other Cats' hair swelled up, and they
seemed on the point of flying at the stranger. The
Rats fled in terror, and the little Birds fluttered on
their perches with fear.

A priest of Lucerne, I don't know how many
hundred years ago, taught a Dog, Cat, Mouse and
Sparrow, to eat out of the same plate. There is
also a somewhat unsatisfactory legend of a maiden
lady who induced twenty-two different animals to
live together upon friendly terms.

Lemmery shut up a Cat and several Mice together in a cage. The Mice in time got to be very
friendly, and plucked and nibbled at their feline

friend. When any of them grew troublesome, she would gently box their ears. A German magazine tells us of a M. Hecart, who tamed a wild Cat and placed a tame sparrow under its protection. Another Cat attacked the Sparrow, which was at the most critical moment rescued by its protector. During the Sparrow's subsequent illness, the Cat watched over it with great tenderness. The same authority gives an instance of a Cat trained like a watch dog, to keep guard over a yard containing a Hare, and some Sparrows, Blackbirds and Partridges.

Captain Marryat, in his amusing way, relates this anecdote. A little black spaniel had five puppies, which were considered too many for her to bring up. As, however, the breed was much in request, her mistress was unwilling that any of them should be destroyed, and asked the cook whether she thought it would be possible to bring a portion of them up by hand before the kitchen fire. In reply, the cook observed that the Cat had that day littered, and that, perhaps, two puppies might be substituted. The Cat made no objection, took to them kindly, and gradually all the kittens were taken away, and the Cat nursed the two puppies only. Now the first curiosity was, that the two puppies nursed by the

Cat were, in a fortnight, as active, forward, and playful as kittens would have been ; they had the use of their legs, basked and gambolled about ; while the other three, nursed by the mother, were whining and rolling about like fat slugs. The Cat gave them her tail to play with, and they were always in motion ; they soon ate meat, and long before the others they were fit to be removed. This was done, and the Cat became very inconsolable. She prowled about the house, and on the second day of tribulation, fell in with the little spaniel who was nursing the other puppies.

" Oh !" says Puss, putting up her back, " it is you who have stolen my children."

" No !" replied the Spaniel, with a snarl ; " they are my own flesh and blood."

" That won't do," said the Cat ; " I'll take my oath, before any Justice of the Peace, that you have my two babies."

Thereupon issue was joined—that is to say, there was a desperate combat, which ended in the defeat of the Spaniel, and in the Cat walking off proudly with one of the puppies, which she took to her own bed. Having deposited this one, she returned, fought again, gained another victory, and bore off another puppy. Now, it is very singular that she should have only taken two, the exact number she had been deprived of.

A lady had a tortoiseshell Cat and a black and white one. A few years ago, the latter was observed to carry her kitten, when two or three days old, to her companion, who brought it up with her own kitten, though of a different age, with all the tenderness of a mother. This was done time after time, for several years ; but last year it was reversed, the black and white Cat taking her turn to discharge the duties of wet-nurse to the kitten of the other. It is probable that a deficiency of milk was the cause of the Cats not suckling their young.

I find in the *Leisure Hour* this story :—

"A lady of the writer's acquaintance was once walking amid the scenery of the Isle of Wight, when she observed a little kitten curled up on a mossy bank, in all the security of a mid-day nap. It was a beautiful little creature, and the lady gently approached, in order to stroke it, when suddenly down swooped a hawk, pounced upon the sleeping kitten, and completely hid it from her sight. It was a kestrel : our friend was greatly shocked, and tried to rescue the little victim ; but the kestrel stood at bay and refused to move. There he stood on the bank, firmly facing her, and all her efforts to drive him from his prey failed. The lady hurried on to a fisherman's cottage, which was near at hand, and told of the little tragedy with the eloquence of real feeling.

" But the fisher-folk were not so disconcerted, and, laughing, said—

" ' It is always so ; that hawk always comes down if anybody goes near the kitten. He has taken to the kitten, and he stays near at hand to watch whenever it goes to sleep.'

" The case was so remarkable that the lady enquired further into its history, and learned that the kitten's mother had died, and that the fisherman's family had missed the little nurseling. After some time, they observed a kestrel hawk loitering about the cottage : they used to throw him scraps of meat, and they noticed that he always carried off a portion of every meal, dragging even heavy bones away out of sight. His movements were watched, and they saw that he carried the stores to the roof of a cottage. A ladder was placed, some one ascended, and there, nestling in a hole in the thatch, lay the lost kitten, thriving prosperously under the tender care of its strange foster-father. The foundling was brought down, and restored to civilized life, but the bandit-protector was not disposed to resign his charge, and ever kept at hand to fly to the rescue whenever dangerous ladies threatened it with a caress."

The following instance of maternal courage and affection is recorded in the *Naturalists' Cabinet :—*

"A Cat that had a numerous brood of kittens, encouraged her little ones to frolic one summer day in the sunshine, at a stable-door. A hawk sailing by, saw them : swift as lightning it darted down on one of the kittens, and would have carried it off, but the mother, seeing its danger, sprang upon the common enemy, which, to defend itself, let fall the prize. The battle that followed was terrible, for the hawk, by the power of his wings, the sharpness of his talons, and the keenness of his beak, had for awhile the advantage, cruelly lacerating the poor Cat, and had actually deprived her of one eye in the conflict ; but Puss, no way daunted by this accident, strove with all her cunning and agility for her little ones, till she had broken the wing of her adversary. In this state she got him more within the power of her claws, the hawk still defending himself apparently with additional vigour ; and the fight continued with equal fury on the side of Grimalkin, to the great entertainment of many spectators. At length, victory seemed to favour the nearly exhausted mother, and she availed herself of the advantage ; for, by an instantaneous exertion, she laid the hawk motionless beneath her feet, and, as if exulting in the victory, tore off the head of the vanquished tyrant. Disregarding the loss of her eye, she immediately ran to the bleeding kitten, licked the wounds inflicted by the hawk's talons on its tender sides, purring while she caressed her liberated offspring, with the same maternal affection as if no danger had assailed them or their affectionate parent."

A lady writer says :—

"Soon after I came to Middlehill, a small tortoise-shell Cat met my children on the road, and followed them home. They, of course, when they saw her, petted and stroked her, and showed their inclination to become friends. She is one of the smallest and most active of full grown Cats I ever saw. From the first she gave evidences of being of a wild and predatory disposition, and made sad havoc among the rabbits, squirrels, and birds. I have several times seen her carrying along a rabbit half as big as herself. Many would exclaim, that, for so nefarious a deed, she ought to have been shot ; but I confess to having the feelings of the unsophisticated Arab, the descendant of

Ishmael, and as she had tasted of my salt, and taken refuge under my roof, besides being the pet of my children, I could not bring myself to order her destruction. Before this we had discovered her lawful owner, a poor cottager, and had sent her back ; but each time that she was sent away, she returned to our porch ; so we made her by purchase legitimately ours. She seemed to be aware of the transaction, and from that time became perfectly at home, and adopted civilised habits, though she still continued very frequently to indulge in a rabbit-hunt. I had added a fine dog to my establishment, to act as a watchman over the wood yard and stables. She and he were at first on fair terms,—a sort of armed neutrality. In process of time, however, she became the mother of a litter of kittens. With the exception of one, they shared the fate of other kittens. When she discovered the loss of her hopeful family, she wandered about looking for them, in a very melancholy way, till, encountering the dog Carlo, it seemed suddenly to strike her that he had been guilty of that act of barbarous spoliation. With back up, she approached, and flew at him with the greatest fury, till blood dropped from his nose, and though ten times

her size, he fairly turned tail and fled. Her surviving
kitten was the very picture of herself, and inherit-
ing also all her predatory habits; when it grew up,
I was obliged to give it away. It left the house in
the neighbouring town to which I sent it, however,
and was afterwards seen domesticated in a stable
yard. Pussy and Carlo now became friends again;
at least, they never interfered with each other.
Pussy, however, to her cost, still continued her
hunting expeditions. The rabbits had committed
great depredations in the garden, and the gardener
had procured two rabbit-traps; one had been set
a considerable distance from the house, and fixed
securely in the ground. One morning, the nurse
heard a plaintive mewing at the nursery window.
She opened it, and in crawled poor Pussy, dragging
the heavy iron rabbit-trap, in the teeth of which
her fore foot was caught. I was called in, and
assisted to release her; her paw swelled, and for
some days she could not move out of the basket
in which she was placed before the fire. Though
suffering intense pain, she must have perceived that
the only way to release herself, was to dig up the
trap, and then she must have dragged her heavy
clog up many steep paths to the room where she
knew her kindest friends, nurse and the children,

for whom she had the greatest affection, were to be
found.   Carlo was caught before in the same trap,
and he bit at it and at everything around, and
severely injured the gardener who went to release
him, biting his arm and legs, and tearing his trousers
to shreds.   Thus, Pussy, under precisely the same
circumstances, showed by far the greatest amount
of sagacity and cool courage.   She, however, not
many weeks afterwards, came in one day with her
foot sadly lacerated, having again got caught in a
trap.   So although she could reason, she did not
appear to have learned wisdom from experience.
She was for long a cripple ; perhaps this last mis-
fortune may have taught her prudence.   Poor thing !
she went limping about the garden, in vain endeavouring, even in the frosty weather, to catch
birds."

I know of a young man who was accustomed to
leave home on a Monday morning and return on
the Saturday, and who had a Cat that used to
come home a few moments after him, and watch
him wash and dress himself, and then sleep on
his clothes until the following Monday, when soon
after the young man went away, the Cat would
go too, and not return all the week.

I also know of a Cat that once rushed into a

house, and took her seat between the master and
mistress while they were at tea ; from that time she
took up her abode with them, and every afternoon
a hamper in which she slept, was heard to creak in
a cellar below, and she would come up and partake of their afternoon meal.

You have all heard of dog-stealers selling a dog
and afterwards stealing it from the purchaser, so
as to sell it again to some other person ; but I
have had a story told me, upon good authority, of
a certain dishonest owner of a very curiously
marked French Cat, who made quite a nice little
income by selling his feline property to the ladies
in his neighbourhood.

You see Pussy had no notion of what an un-
principled ruffian he was, nor what was the nature
of the contract between him and her other owners.
She loved him very much, and fretted in her new
home, waited impatiently for an opportunity, and
at last, finding the door open, returned to her
robber master rejoicing.

He, worthy creature, also rejoiced at sight of
her, and hugged her to his manly breast. Then
he gave her some nice warm milk, and a large
slice of meat. Next day he sold her again, if he
got a chance.

This little game went on very comfortably for some months, and might have gone on longer, had it not been for an awkward mistake. An old lady, who had been one of the purchasers of the Cat, changed her residence, and our ingenious friend, unaware of the circumstance, called upon her again, and tried to re-sell her the animal; thereupon, some unpleasantness occurred, and I believe the Cat-merchant got into trouble.

CHAPTER IX.

—o—

Of Puss in Proverbs, in the Dark Ages, and in the Company of Wicked Old Women.

—o—

THESE are some of the best known Proverbs about Cats:—

"Care will kill a Cat," one says, and yet Cats are said to have nine lives. Let us hope that poor Pussy will never be put to a worse death.

"A muffled Cat is no good mouser."

"That Cat is out of kind that sweet milk will not lap."

"You can have no more of a Cat than her skin." This proverb seems to refer to the unfitness of her flesh for food. Formerly the fur of the Cat was used in trimming coats and cloaks. The Cat-gut used for rackets, and for the fine strings of violins, is made from the dried intestines of the Cat, the larger strings being from the intestines of sheep and lambs.

"Fain would the Cat fish eat, but she is loth to wet her feet."

"The Cat sees not the mouse ever."

"When the Cat winketh, little wots the mouse what the Cat thinketh."

"Though the Cat winks a while, yet sure she is not blind."

"Well might the Cat wink when both her eyes were out?"

"How can the Cat help it, if the maid be a fool?" Which means how can it help breaking or stealing that which is left in its way?

"That that comes of a Cat will catch mice."

"A Cat may look at a king."

"An old Cat laps as much as a young kitten."

"When the Cat is away, the mice will play."

"When candles are out, all Cats are grey." Otherwise, "Joan is as good as my Lady in the dark."

" The Cat knows whose lips she licks."

" Cry you mercy, killed my Cat." This is spoken to those who play one a trick, and then try to escape punishment by begging pardon.

" By biting and scratching, Cats and Dogs come together."

" I'll keep no more Cats than will catch mice ;" or no more in family than will earn their living.

" Who shall hang the bell about the Cat's neck." The mice at a consultation, how to secure themselves from the Cat, resolved upon hanging a bell about her neck, to give warning when she approached ; but when this was resolved on, they were as far off as ever, for who was to do it ? John Skelton says :—

> " But they are lothe to mel,
> And lothe to hang the bel
> About the Catte's neck,
> Fro dred to have a checke"

" A Cat has nine lives, and a woman has nine Cats' lives."

" Cats eat what hussies spare."

" Cats hide their claws."

" The wandering Cat gets many a rap."

" The Cat is hungry when a crust contents her."

M

" He lives under the sign of the *Cat's foot ;*" that is to say, he is hen-pecked — his wife scratches him.

Here are some French proverbs :—

" Chat échaudé craint l'eau froide." (A burnt child dreads the fire.)

" Ne réveillons pas les Chats qui dort." (Let sleeping dogs alone.)

" La nuit tous Chats sont gris."

Molière says :—

" Vous êtes-vous mis dans la tête que Léonard de Pourceaugnac soit un homme à acheter Chat en poche." (To buy a pig in a poke.)

" Ce n'est pas à moi que l'on vendra un Chat pour un lièvre." (Don't think you can catch an old bird with chaff.)

" Elle est friande comme une chatte." (She's as dainty as a Cat.)

" Payer en Chats et en rats." (To pay in driblets.)

" Appeler un Chat un Chat." (Call a spade a spade.)

" Avoir un Chat dans la gorge." (Something sticking in the throat.)

Shakespeare says :—

> " Letting ' I dare not' wait upon ' I would,'
> Like the poor Cat i'the adage."

Again :—

> " Let Hercules himself do what he may,
> The Cat will mew, and Dog will have his day."

The wisdom of our forefathers teaches us, that if a Cat be carried in a bag from its old home to a new house, let the distance be several miles, it will be certain to return again ; but if it be carried backward into the new house this will not be the case.

A Cat's eyes wax and wane as the moon waxes and wanes, and the course of the sun is followed by the apples of its eyes.

The brain of a Cat may be used as a love spell if taken in small doses.

If a man swallow two or three Cat's hairs, it will cause him to faint. As a cure for epilepsy, take three drops of blood from under a Cat's tail in water.

The horse ridden by a man who has got any Cat's hair on his clothing will perspire violently, and soon become exhausted. If the wind blows over a Cat riding in a vehicle, upon the horse drawing it, it will weary the horse very much.

To preserve your eyesight, burn the head of a

black Cat to ashes, and have a little of the dust blown into your eyes three times a day.

To cure a whitlow, put the finger affected a quarter of an hour every day into a Cat's ear.

The fat of the wild Cat (Axungia Cati Sylvestris) is good for curing epilepsy and lameness. The skin of the wild Cat worn as coverings, will give strength to the limbs.

Now about dreams :—

If any one dreams that he hath encountered a Cat, or killed one, he will commit a thief to prison and prosecute him to the death, for the Cat signifies a common thief. If he dreams that he eats Cat's flesh, he will have the goods of the thief that robbed him ; if he dreams that he hath the skin, then he will have all the thief's goods. If any one dreams he fought with a Cat that scratched him sorely, that denotes some sickness or affliction. If any shall dream that a woman became the mother of a Cat instead of a well shaped baby, it is a bad hieroglyphic, and betokens no good to the dreamer.

Stevens states, that in some counties of England, it used to be thought a good bit of fun to close up a Cat in a cask with a quantity of soot, and suspend the cask on a line ; then he who could knock out the bottom of the cask as he ran under it, and was nimble enough to escape its falling contents, was thought to be very clever. After the first part had been performed, the Cat was hunted to death, which finished this diverting pastime. They were full of their fun, once upon a time, in merrie England.

In an old-fashioned treatise upon Rat-catching, I find mentioned a means of alluring " of very material efficacy, which is, the use of oil of Rhodium, which, like the marumlyriacum, in the case of Cats, has a very extraordinary fascinating power on these animals."

Among the sympathetic secrets in occult philosophy, published in the *Conjurors' Magazine*, in 1791, I find a recipe " to draw Cats together, and fascinate them," which is as follows :—

" In the new moon, gather the herb Nepe, and dry it in the heat of the sun, when it is temperately hot : gather vervain in the hour ☿, and only expose it to the air while ☉ is under the earth. Hang these together in a net, in a convenient place, and when one of them has scented it, her cry will soon call those about her that are within hearing ; and they will rant and run about, leaping and capering to get at the net, which must be hung or placed so that they cannot easily accomplish it, for they will certainly tear it to pieces. Near Bristol there is a field that goes by the appellation of the 'Field of Cats,' from a large number of these animals being drawn together there by this contrivance."

One of the frauds of witchcraft was the witch pretending to transform herself into a Cat, and this led to the Cat being tormented by the ignorant vulgar.

In 1618, Margaret and Philip Flower were executed at Lincoln ; their mother was also accused, dying in goal before (probably of fright, added to old age and infirmity). It was asserted that they had procured the death of the Lord Henry Mosse, eldest son of the Earl of Rutland, by procuring his right-hand glove, which, after being rubbed on the back of their imp, named " Rutterkin," and which lived with them in the form of a Cat, was plunged into boiling water, pricked with a knife, and buried in a dung-hill, so that, as that rotted, the liver of the young man might rot also, which was affirmed to have come to pass.

Those were dreadful times for the ill-looking old ladies, and the more so if they were unfortunate enough to have an affection for the feline race.

" A wrinkled hag, of wicked fame,
  Beside a little smoky flame,
  Sat hovering, pinched with age and frost,
  Her shrivelled hands with veins embossed.
  Upon her knees her weight sustains,
  While palsy shook her crazy brains ;
  She mumbles forth her backward prayer—
  An untamed scold of fourscore year.
  About her swarmed a numerous brood
  Of Cats, who, lank with hunger, mewed ;
  Teased with their cries, her choler grew,
  And thus she sputtered—' Hence, ye crew !
  Fool that I was to entertain
  Such imps, such fiends—a hellish train ;
  Had ye been never housed and nursed,
  I for a witch had n'er been cursed ;
  To you I owe that crowd of boys
  Worry me with eternal noise ;—
  Straws laid across, my pace retard ;
  The horse-shoes nailed (each threshold's guard) ;
  The stunted broom the wenches hide,
  For fear that I should up and ride.' "

The belief in witchcraft is a very ancient and deep-rooted one. From the earliest times, we can trace records of supposed acts of witchcraft, and their punishment. Pope Innocent VIII., in 1484, issued a bull, empowering the Inquisition to search for witches and burn them. From the time of this superstitious act, the executions for witchcraft increased. The pope had given sanction to the belief in this demoniacal power, and had asserted their possession of it. In 1485, forty-one poor women were burnt as witches in Germany; an inquisitor in Piedmont burnt a hundred more, and was proceeding so fast with others daily, that the people rose *en masse*, and chased him out of the country. About the same time, five hundred witches were executed at Geneva, in the course of three months.

Among the many who counterfeited possession by the devil, for the purpose of attracting pity or obtaining money, were Agnes Bridges and Rachel Pinder, who had counterfeited to be possessed by the devil, and vomited pins and rags; but were detected, and stood before the preacher at St. Paul's Cross, and acknowledged their hypocritical coun-terfeiting : this happened in 1574.

In fifteen years, from 1580 to 1595, Remigius burnt nine hundred reputed witches in Lorraine. In Germany, they tortured and burnt them daily, until many unfortunates destroyed themselves for fear of a death by torment, and others fled the country.

Ludovicus Paramo states, that the Inquisition, within the space of 150 years, had burnt thirty thousand of these reputed witches.

The superstition continued on the increase, and reached its culmination in the Puritanic time of the Commonwealth, when persons more cunning and wicked than the rest, gained a subsistence by discovering witches (by pretended marks and trials they used), and denouncing them to death. The chief of these persons was MATHEW HOPKINS, *Witch Finder General*, as he termed himself. He was a native of Manningtree, in Essex, and he devoted his pretended powers so zealously in the service of his country, that in 1644, sixteen witches, discovered by him, were burnt at Yarmouth; fifteen were condemned at Chelmsford, and hanged in that town and at Manningtree. Many more at Bury St. Edmunds, in 1645 and 1646, amounting to nearly forty in all at the several places of execution, and as many more in the country as made up threescore.

In this work he was aided by one John Stern, and a woman, who with the rest, pretended to have secret means of testing witchcraft; nor was their zeal unrewarded by the weak and superstitious parliament. Mr. Hopkins, in a book published in 1647, owns that he had twenty shillings for each town he visited to discover witches, and owns that he punished many: testing them

by a water ordeal, to see if they would sink or
swim.   He says that he swam many, and watched
them for four nights together, keeping them standing or walking till their feet were blistered ; " the
reason" as he says, " was to prevent their couching
down ; for indeed, when they be suffered to couch,
immediately come their familiars in the room, and
scareth the watchers, and heartneth (encourageth)
the witch."

This swimming experiment, which was deemed
a full proof of guilt if any one subjected to it did
not sink, but floated on the surface of the water,
was one of the ordeals especially recommended
by our king, James I., who, in a work upon the
subject, among other things, assigned this somewhat ridiculous reason for its pretended infallibi-
lity:—" That as such persons had renounced their
baptism by water, so the water refuses to receive
them."   Consequently, those who were accused
of diabolical practices, were tied neck and heels
together, and tossed into a pond ; if they floated
or swam they were guilty, and therefore taken
out and hanged or burnt ; if they were innocent,
they were drowned. Of this method of trial by
water ordeal, Scot observes : "that a woman above
the age of fifty years, and being bound both hand

and foot, her clothes being upon her, and being laid softly upon the water, sinketh not a long time, some say not at all." And Dr. Hutchinson confirms this, by saying, not one in ten even sink in that position of their bodies. Its utter fallacy was shown when the witch finders themselves were thus tested ; and the last quoted writer says, that if the books written against witchcraft were tested by the same ordeal, they would in no degree come off more safely.

One of the most cruel cases was that of Mr. Lowes, a clergyman, who had reached the patriarchal age of eighty. He was one of those unfortunate ministers of the Gospel whose livings were sequestered by the parliament, and who was suspected as malignant because he preserved his loyalty and the homilies of the Church. It would have been well for him had this been the only suspicion ; but he was accused of witchcraft ; and it was asserted that he had sunk ships at sea by the power he possessed, and witnesses were found who swore to seeing him do it. He was seized and tested. They watched him, and kept him awake at night, and ran him backwards and forwards about the room until he was out of breath ; then they rested him a little, and then ran him again. And thus they did for several days and nights together, until he was weary of his life, and was scarce sensible of what he said or did. They swam him twice or thrice, although that was no true rule to try him by, for they sent in unsuspected people at the same time, and they swam as well as he; yet was the unfortunate old clergyman condemned to death and executed.

In the book written some years after this, by Mr. Gaul, he mentions their mode of discovering witches, which was principally by marks or signs upon their bodies, which were in reality but moles, scorbutic spots, or warts, which frequently grow large and pendulous in old age, and were absurdly declared to be teats to suckle imps. Thus of one, Joane Willimot, in 1619, it was sworn that she had two imps, one in the form of a kitten, and another in that of a mole, " and they leapt on her shoulder, and the kitten sucked under her right ear, on her neck, and the mole on the left side, in the like place ; " and at another time a spirit was seen " sucking her under the left ear, in the likeness of a little white dogge." (See *The Wonderful Discovery of the Witchcrafts of Margare and Philip Flower*, 1619).

Another test was to place the suspected witch in

the middle of a room, upon a stool or table, cross-legged, or in some other uneasy posture, and if she were refractory, she was tied too by cords, and kept without meat or sleep for a space of four-and-twenty hours ; all this time she was strictly watched, because it was believed that in the course of that time her imp would come to suck her, for whom some hole or ingress was provided. The watchers swept the room frequently, so that nothing might escape them ; and should a fly or spider be found that had the activity to elude them, they were assured these were the imps. In 1645 one was hanged at Cambridge, who kept a tame frog which was sworn to be her imp ; and one at Gloucester, in 1649, who was convicted for having suckled a sow in the form of a little black creature. In "a Tryal of Witches, at Bury St. Edmunds, 1664," a witness deposed to having caught one of these imps in a blanket, waiting for her child, who slept in it and was bewitched ; that it was in the form of a toad, and was caught and thrown into the fire, where " it made a great and horrible noise, and after a space there was a flashing in the fire like gunpowder, making a noise like the discharge of a pistol, and thereupon the toad was no more seen nor heard." All of which was the simple natural result of this cruel proceeding, but which was received by judge and jury, at that time, of the poor toad being an imp !

Hutchinson, in his essay on witchcraft, says :— " It was very requisite that these witch-finders should take care to go to no towns but where they might do what they would without being controlled by sticklers ; but if the times had not been as they were, they would have found but few towns where they might be suffered to use the trial of the stool, which was as bad as most tortures. Do but imagine a poor old creature, under all the weakness and infirmities of old age, set like a fool in the middle of a room, with a rabble of ten towns about her home ; then her legs tied across, that all the weight of her body might rest upon her seat. By that means, after some hours, the circulation of the blood would be stopped, and her sitting would be as painful as the wooden horse· Then must she continue in pain four-and-twenty hours, without either sleep or meat ; and since this was their ungodly way of trial, what wonder was it if, when they were weary of their lives, they confessed many tales that would please them, and many times they knew not what."

Hopkins' favourite and ultimate method of

proof was by swimming, as before narrated. They tied together the thumbs and toes of the suspected person, about whose waist was fastened a cord, the ends of which were held on the banks of the river by two men, whose power it was to strain or slacken it. If they floated, they were witches. After a considerable course of wicked accusation on the part of Hopkins and his accomplices, testing all by these modes of trial, and ending in the cruel deaths of many wretched old persons, a reaction against him took place, probably at the instigation of some whose friends had been condemned innocently, or of those who were too wise to believe in his tests, and disgusted with his cold wickedness. His own famous and conclusive evidence—the experiment of swimming—was tried *upon himself*; and this wretch, who had sacrificed so many, by the same test, was found to be *guilty*, too. He was deservedly con-demned, and suffered death himself as a wizard."

Dr. Harsenet, Archbishop of York, in his *Declaration of Popish Impostures*, says, " Out of those is shap'd us the true idea of a witch, an old weather-beaten crone, having her chin and knees meeting for age, walking like a bow leaning on a staff, hollow ey'd, untooth'd, furrow'd on her face, having her lips trembling with the palsy, going

mumbling in the streets—one that hath forgotten
her pater-noster, and yet hath a shrewd tongue to
call a drab a drab!—if she hath learned of an
old wife in a chimney end, pax, max, fax, for a
spell, or can say Sir John Grantham's curse for
a nuller's eels—' All ye that have stolen the miller's
eels, Laudate Dominum de Cœlis, and they that
have consented thereto, Benedicamus Domino,' why
then, beware, look about you, my neighbours. If
any of you have a sheep sick of the giddies, or a
hog of the mumps, or a horse of the staggers, or
a knavish boy of the school, or an idle girl of the
wheel, or a young drab of the sullens, and hath not
fat enough for her porridge, or butter enough for
her bread, and she hath a little help of the epilepsy
or cramp to teach her to roll her eyes, wry her
mouth, gnash her teeth, startle with her body, hold
her arms and hands stiff, etc. And then, when an
old Mother Nobs hath by chance called her 'idle
young housewife,' or bid the devil scratch her, then
no doubt but Mother Nobs is the witch, and the
young girl is owl-blasted, etc. They that have
their brains baited, and their fancies distempered,
with the imaginations and apprehensions of witches,
conjurors, and fairies, and all that lymphatical
chimera, I find to be marshalled in one of these

five ranks :—Children, fools, women, cowards, sick
or black melancholic discomposed wits."

Many hundreds of poor old women, and many a
Cat, were sacrificed to the zealous Master Hopkins,
for Cats and Kittens were frequently said to be
imps, who had taken that form. However, he was
not the only scoundrel who made witch-finding a
trade.

In Syke's *Local Recorder*, mention is made of a
Scotchman, who pretended great powers of discovering witchcraft, and was engaged by the towns-
men of Newcastle to practise there ; and one man
and fifteen women were hanged by him. But he
ultimately shared, as Hopkins did, the cruel fate
he had awarded to so many others. " When the
witch-finder had done in Newcastle, and received
his wages, he went into Northumberland to try
women there, and got three pounds a-piece ; but
Henry Doyle, Esq., laid hold on him, and required
bond of him to answer at the Sessions. He
escaped into Scotland, where he was made prisoner,
indicted, arraigned, and condemned for such-like
villany exercised in Scotland, and confessed at the
gallows that he had been the death of above two
hundred and twenty women in England and Scotland."

Here is an account of the death of a famous witch's famous Cat :—

> " Ye rats, in triumph elevate your ears !
>   Exult, ye mice ! for Fate's abhorred shears
>   Of Dick's nine lives have slit the Cat-guts nine ;
>   Henceforth he mews 'midst choirs of Cats divine !"

So sings Mr. Huddesford, in a " Monody on the death of Dick, an Academical Cat," with this motto :—

> " Mi-Cat inter omnes."
>
> *Hor. Carm.*, Lib. i., Ode 12.

He brings his Cat, Dick, from the Flood, and consequently through Rutterkin, a Cat who was " cater-cousin to the great-great-great-great-great-great-great-great-grandmother of Grimalkin, and first Cat in the Caterie of an old woman, who was tried for bewitching a daughter of the Countess of Rutland, in the beginning of the sixteenth century." The monodist connects him with Cats of great renown in the annals of witchcraft ; a science whereto they have been allied as closely as poor old women, one of whom, it appears, on the authority of an old pamphlet, entitled " *Mewes from Scotland*," etc., printed in the year 1591, " confessed

that she took a Cat and christened it, etc., and that
in the night following, the said Cat was conveyed
into the middest of the sea by all these witches
sayling in their riddles, or cives, so left the said
Cat right before the towne of Leith, in Scotland.
This done, there did arise such a tempest at sea,
as a greater hath not been seen since. Againe it
is confessed that the said christened Cat was the
cause of the Kinge's majestie's shippe, at his
coming forthe of Denmark, had a contrarie winde
to the rest of the shippes then being in his com-
panie, which thing was most straunge and true, as
the Kinge's Majestie acknowledgeth, for when the
rest of the shippes had a fair and good winde, then
was the winde contrarie, and altogether against his
Majestie," etc.

All sorts of Cats, according to Huddesford,
lamented the death of his favourite, whom he calls
" premier Cat upon the catalogue," and who, pre-
ferring sprats to all other fish—

> " Had swallow'd down a score, without remorse,
> And three fat mice slew for a second course ;
> But, while the third his grinders dyed with gore,
> Sudden those grinders clos'd—to grind no more !
> And, dire to tell ! commission'd by old Nick,
> A catalepsy made an end of Dick.

Calumnious Cats, who circulate *faux pas*,
And reputations maul with murderous claws ;
Shrill Cats, whom fierce domestic brawls delight,
Cross Cats, who nothing want but teeth to bite ;
Starch Cats of puritanic aspect sad,
And learned Cats, who talk their husbands mad ;
Confounded Cats, who cough, and croak, and cry,
And maudlin Cats who drink eternally ;
Fastidious Cats, who pine for costly cates,
And jealous Cats who catechise their mates ;
Cat prudes who, when they're ask'd the question, squall,
And ne'er give answer categorical ;
Uncleanly Cats, who never pare their nails,
Cat-gossips, full of Canterbury tales ;
Cat-grandams, vex'd with asthmas and catarrhs,
And superstitious Cats, who curse their stars ;
Cats of each class, craft, calling, and degree,
Mourn Dick's calamitous catastrophe !
Yet while I chant the cause of Richard's end,
Ye sympathising Cats, your tears suspend !
Then shed enough to float a dozen whales,
And use for pocket handkerchiefs your tails !
Ah ! though thy bust adorn no sculptur'd shrine,
No vase thy relics rare to fame consign ;
No rev'rend characters thy rank express,
Nor hail thee, Dick, ' D.D. nor F.R.S.'
Though no funereal cypress shade thy tomb,
For thee the wreaths of Paradise shall bloom ;
There, while Grimalkin's mew her Richard greets,
A thousand Cats shall purr on purple seats.
E'en now I see, descending from his throne,
Thy venerable Cat, O Whittington !
The kindred excellence of Richard hail,
And wave with joy his gratulating tail !

> There shall the worthies of the whiskered race
> Elysian mice o'er floors of sapphire chase,
> Midst beds of aromatic marum stray,
> Or raptur'd rove beside the milky way.
> Kittens, than eastern houris fairer seen,
> Whose bright eyes glisten with immortal green,
> Shall smooth for tabby swains their yielding fur,
> And, to their amorous mews, assenting purr ;—
> There, like Alcmena's, shall Grimalkin's son
> In bliss repose,—his mousing labours done,
> Fate, envy, curs, time, tide, and traps defy,
> And caterwaul to all eternity."

To conclude this Chapter, an incident which took place only a few days ago, in Essex, at a village within forty miles of London, and which came under the personal knowledge of the writer, may be adduced, to show that, however witchcraft may have been laughed away—and laughter has been more effectual to rid the world of it than rope or stake—there are still to be found individuals who believe in the evil powers of hook-nosed crones, black Cats, and broom-sticks.

In a squalid hut lived a miserable dame, whose only claims to a demoniacal connection were her excessive age and her sombre Cat. Whether the neighbours thought the Cat was more of a witch than the woman, or whether they had a wholesome dread of the punishment inflicted upon murderers,

it was upon the *animal* the bewitched ones determined to wreak their vengeance, and then it was
that the true satanic nature of poor Puss appeared.
Traps were set to catch her, but she would not be
caught; ropes were purchased to hang her, but she
would not bow her head to the noose; and, finally,
a blunderbuss was loaded to shoot her—loaded to
the very muzzle. By conjurations and enchant-
ments, when that gun was fired, it knocked the
holder backwards, and never injured the black Cat.
Another man tried, with the same result, and yet
another. It was evident the gun was bewitched, so
Pussy's murder was given up for the time, and,
with the exception of the tip of her tail, lost in
one of the traps, passed the remainder of her life
happy and unmutilated.

CHAPTER X.

CHAPTER X

—o—

*Of a certain Voracious Cat, some
Goblin Cats, Magical Cats,
and Cats of Kilkenny.*

—o—

OF all the great
big stories that
have been told
of Cats, that
which describes the origin
of Cat's-head apples is surely the greatest biggest
one. The legend runs thus :—

" The Widow Tomkins had a back room, on the second floor ;
 Her name was on a neat brass plate on one side of the door :
 Companion she had only one—a beautiful Tom Cat,
 Who was a famous mouser, the dickens for a rat :

His colour was a tabby, and his skin as soft as silk,
And she would lap him every day while he lapped the milk.
One day she was disturbed from sleep with double rat-tat-tat,
And she went in such a hurry that she quite forgot her Cat.

*   *   *   *

Poor Thomas, soon as day-light came, walked up and down the
    floor,
And heard the dogs'-meat woman cry "Cats'-meat" at the door ;
With hunger he got fairly wild, though formerly so tame—
Another day passed slowly, another just the same.
With hunger he so hungry was—it did so strong assail,
That, although very loath, he was obliged to eat his tail.
This whetted quite his appetite, and though his stump was sore,
The next day he was tempted (sad) to eat a little more.
To make his life the longer then, he made his body shorter,
And one after the other attacked each hinder quarter.
He walked about on two fore legs, alas ! without beholders,
'Till more and more by hunger pressed, he dined on both his
    shoulders.
Next day he found (the cannibal !) to eating more a check,
Although he tried, and did reach all he could reach of his neck.
But as he could not bite his ear, all mournfully he cried,—
Towards the door he turned his eyes, cocked up his nose, and died.
The widow did at last return, and oh ! how she did stare,
She guessed the tale as soon as she saw Tom's head lying there.
Quite grief sincerely heart-felt as she owned his fate a hard'un,
She buried it beneath an apple-tree just down her garden.
So mark what strange effects from little causes will appear,
The fruit of this said tree was changed, and strangely, too, next
    year.
The neighbours say ('tis truth, for they're folks who go to chapels),
This Cat's head was the sole first cause of all the Cat's-head
    apples !"

THE CAT AND THE CONJUROR.

Page 187.

Gottfried Heller, in *Die Leute von Seldwyla,* tells a droll story. This is an abridgement of a popular author's version of it, published some years ago :—

" One day, once upon a time, or thereabouts, the witch-finder of a certain Swiss town — himself secretly a wizard—was taking his afternoon's walk, when he came across a Tom Cat, looking very thin and miserable. This Cat had once been the chief favourite of a rich old lady, who had trained him up in luxurious living. Now she was dead, and Tom's happy days were over : he was as shaggy and meagre, as he had formerly been sleek and plump. Now, you must know that Cats' grease was, in those days, an invaluable ingredient for certain magical preparations, provided the Cat to whom it belonged willingly made a donation of it. This proviso rendered good efficient Cats' grease an exceedingly rare commodity ; for though there might be no great difficulty in finding a fat Cat, to find one willing to part with its fat was, of course, difficult enough.

" Here, however, was an animal in desperate circumstances, who might be accessible to reason ; therefore, says the magician—

" ' How much will you take for your fat ?'

" ' Why, I haven't got any,' replied Tom, who, to tell the truth, was as thin as a hurdle.

" ' You may have, though, if you say the word,' said the magician ; 'and I'll tell you how.'

" You see, he knew from experience that Tom was a Cat who was capable of making flesh, for he had known him as round as a dumpling ; so he made this bargain :—' He offered Tom a whole month's luxurious living on condition that at the expiration of that time he should voluntarily lay down his life and yield up all the fat he had acquired during the four weeks. Of course Tom agreed, and the contract was signed on the spot. The apartment provided for Tom's lodging was 'fitted up as an artificial landscape. A little wood was perched on the top of a little mountain, which rose from the banks of a little lake. On the branches of the trees were perched dainty birds, all roasted, and emitting a most savoury odour. From the cavities of the mountain peered forth sundry baked mice, all seasoned with delicious stuffing and exquisitely larded with bacon. The lake consisted of the newest milk, with a small fish or two at the bottom. Thus, to the enjoyment of the epicure, was added the excitement of imaginary sportsmanship. Tom ate his fill, and more, and soon became as fat as the

magician could wish, but before long he became
thoughtful. The month had nearly expired; at the
end he was to die if fat enough. Ah! a bright
thought, he would get thin again. With a won-
drous strength of mind he refrained from eating
the luxuries provided, took plenty of exercise on
the house-tops, and kept himself in excellent
health, but much thinner than suited the wizard's
fancy.

" Before long, this gentleman remonstrated with
Tom, pointing out to him very plainly, that he was
bound by all the laws of honour to get fat by the
month's end. To this, Tom had little to urge of
any moment, and the magician informed him that
he would kill him at the appointed period, let him be
in what condition he might. Tom, therefore, would
gain nothing by being thin, and it was hoped that
his good taste, unchecked by other considerations,
would induce him to make up for lost time. Time
rolled on, Tom behaved worse than ever, and when
the fatal day arrived 'he looked in worse condition
than ever—a dissipated, abandoned, shaggy scamp,
without an ounce on his bones.' The wizard could
not stand this, so he thrust Tom into an empty
coop and fed him by violence. In course of time,
the wizard was satisfied, and began to sharpen his

knife; but no sooner did Tom perceive this act, than he began to utter such singular expressions of contrition, that his proprietor paused to ask him to explain them. The Cat in wild terms alluded to a certain sum of ten thousand florins lying at the bottom of a well, and the wizard wanted to know more about them. It appeared then, that Tom's late mistress had thrown the sum he named to the bottom of a well, and informed her Cat that 'should he find a perfectly beautiful and a penniless maiden, whom a perfectly honest man was inclined to wed in spite of her poverty, then he should empty the contents of the well as a marriage portion.'

"Of course this tale was false. The money existed where Tom had described, but it had been ill-gotten gold, with a curse upon it. But the wizard nibbled at the bait, put a chain round Tom's neck, and went to have a look at the treasure. There it was, sure enough, shining under the water.

" 'Are you quite sure that there are exactly ten thousand florins ?' asked the magician.

" 'I've never been down to see,' replied Tom; ' I was obliged to take the old lady's word for it.'

" 'But where shall I find a wife?' asked the wizard.

" 'I'll find you one,' said Tom.

" 'Will you ?'

" 'To be sure. Tear up that contract, though, to begin with.'

" The wizard, not without grumbling, drew from his pocket the fatal paper, which Tom no sooner perceived than he pounced on it and swallowed it whole, making at the same time the reflection that he had never before tasted so delicious a morsel in his life.

" In the neighbourhood dwelt an old woman, who was a witch—one of the ugliest old women you ever saw, who every night flew up the chimney on a broom-stick, and played Meg's diversions by the light of the moon. This lady had an owl, who was a bird of loose principles, and had been an associate of Tom's in his gay days. This bright couple consulted together how they should persuade the ancient maiden to marry the old man.

" ' She never will,' said the owl.

" ' Then we must make her ; but how ?'

" ' We must catch her first, and take her prisoner, and that is to be done easily enough, with a net, spun by a man of sixty years old, who has never set eyes on the face of woman.'

" ' Where are we to find him ?'

" ' Just round the corner : he has been blind from his birth.'

" When the net had been procured, they set it in
the chimney, and presently caught the old lady,
and after much trouble they starved her into com-
pliance. Then, by magical art, she put on an appearance of youth and beauty, and the wizard
married her in an ecstacy of delight; but was he
not in a fury when, evening approaching, she resumed her pristine ugliness. And was he not disgusted at his bride, in spite of the treasure she had
brought him. As for Tom, like many bad people,
he lived happy ever afterwards."

Here is an abridgement of the famous tale of
Puss in Boots :—

" A miller died, leaving his youngest son nothing
but a Cat : the poor young fellow complained bit-
terly of his fate ; the Cat bade him be of good cheer,
and procure a pair of boots and a bag : the youth
contrived to do so. The first attempt Puss made
was to go into a warren, in which there was a great
number of rabbits. He put some bran and parsley
into his bag ; and then, stretching himself out at
full length, as if he were dead, he waited for some
young rabbits, who as yet knew nothing of the
cunning tricks of the world, to come and get into
the bag. Scarcely had he laid down, before he
succeeded as well as could be wished. A giddy

young rabbit crept into the bag, and the Cat immediately drew the strings, and killed it without mercy. Puss, proud of his prey, hastened directly to the palace, where he asked to speak to the King. On being shown into the apartment of his Majesty, he made a low bow, and said :—" I have brought you, Sire, this rabbit from the warren of my Lord the Marquis of Carabas, who commanded me to present it to your Majesty, with the assurance of his respects." One day, the Cat having heard that the King intended to take a ride that morning by the river's side with his daughter, who was the most beautiful Princess in the world, he said to his master :—" Take off your clothes, and bathe yourself in the river, just in the place I shall show you, and leave the rest to me." The Marquis did exactly as he was desired, without being able to guess at what the Cat intended. While he was bathing, the King passed by, and Puss directly called out, as loudly as he could bawl :—" Help! help! My Lord Marquis of Carabas is in danger of being drowned!" The King hearing the cries, and recognising the Cat, ordered his attendants to go directly to the assistance of my Lord Marquis of Carabas ; and the cunning Cat having hid his master's clothes under a large stone, the King commanded the

O

officers of his wardrobe to fetch him the handsomest
suit it contained. The King's daughter was mightily
taken with his appearance, and the Marquis of
Carabas had no sooner cast upon her two or three
respectful glances, than she became violently in love
with him. The Cat, enchanted to see how well his
scheme was likely to succeed, ran before to a
meadow that was reaping, and said to the reapers :—
" Good people, if you do not tell the King, who will
soon pass this way, that the meadow you are reaping belongs to my Lord Marquis of Carabas, you
shall be chopped as small as mince-meat." The
King did not fail to ask the reapers to whom the
meadow belonged ? " To my Lord Marquis of
Carabas," said they all at once ; for the threats of
the Cat had terribly frightened them. Puss at
length arrived at a stately castle that belonged to
an Ogre, whom he first persuaded to assume the
form of a mouse, and then cleverly gobbled him up
before he could get back to his proper shape again.
The King's party soon after arrived. The Cat said
the castle was his master's ; and the King was so
much charmed with the amiable qualities and noble
fortune of the Marquis of Carabas, and the young
Princess too had fallen so violently in love with
him, that when the King had partaken of a colla-

tion, he said to the Marquis :—" It will be your own fault, my Lord Marquis of Carabas, if you do not soon become my son-in-law." The Marquis received the intelligence with a thousand respectful acknowledgments, accepted the honour conferred upon him, and married the Princess that very day. The Cat became a great lord, and never after pursued rats, except for his own amusement.

I think, too, that the famous story of the *White Cat* should also find a place in this little volume :—

There once was a King, the legend says, who was growing old, and it was told to him that his three sons wished to govern the kingdom. The old King, who did not wish to give up his power just yet, thought the best way to prevent his sons from taking his throne was to send them out to seek for adventures ; so he called them all around him, and said :—

" My sons, go away and travel for a year ; and he of you who brings me the most beautiful little dog, shall have the kingdom, and be King after me."

Then the three Princes started on the journey ; but it is of the youngest of the three that I have now to tell. He travelled for many days, and at last found himself, one evening, at the door of a splendid castle, but not a man or woman was to be seen. A number of hands, with no bodies to them, appeared : two hands took off the Prince's cloak, two others seated him in a chair, another pair brought a brush to brush his hair, and several pairs waited on him at supper. Then some more hands came and put him to bed in a fine chamber, where he slept all night, but still no one appeared. The next morning, the hands brought him into a splendid hall, where there sat on a throne a large White Cat, who made him sit beside her, and expressed herself glad to see him. Next day, the Prince and the White Cat went out hunting together : the Cat was mounted on a fine spirited monkey, and seemed very fond of the Prince, who, on his part, was delighted with her wit and cleverness.

Instead of dogs, Cats hunted for them. These creatures ran with great agility after rats, and mice, and birds, catching and killing a great number of them ; and sometimes the White Cat's monkey would climb a tree, with the White Cat on his back, after a bird, a mouse, or a squirrel. This pleasant life went on for a long time : every day the White Cat became more fond of the Prince, while, on his part, the Prince could not help loving the poor Cat, who was so kind and attentive to him. At last, the time drew near when the Prince was to return home, and he had not thought of looking for a little dog; but the Cat gave him a casket, and told him to open this before the King, and all would be well; so the Prince journeyed home, taking with him an ugly mongrel cur. When the brothers saw this, they laughed secretly to each other, and thought themselves quite secure, so far as their younger brother was concerned. They had, with infinite pains, procured each of them a very rare and beautiful little dog, and each thought himself quite sure to get the prize. When the day came on which the dogs were to be shown, each of the two elder Princes produced a beautiful little dog, on a silk velvet cushion : no one could judge which was the prettier. The youngest now opened his casket, and found a walnut : he cracked this walnut, and out of the walnut sprang a little tiny dog, of exquisite beauty. Still the old King would not give up his kingdom. He told the young Princes they must bring him home a piece of cambric so fine that it could be threaded through the eye of a needle ; and so they went away in search of such a piece of cambric. Again the youngest Prince passed a year with the White Cat, and again the Cat gave him a walnut when the time came for him to return home. The three Princes were summoned before their father, who produced a needle. The first and second Princes brought a piece of cambric which would almost, but not quite, go through the needle's eye. The youngest Prince broke open his walnut-shell : he found inside it a small nut-shell, and then a cherry-stone, and then a grain of wheat, and then a grain of millet, and in this grain of millet a piece of cambric four hundred yards long, which passed easily through the eye of the needle. But the old King said :—

"He who brings the most beautiful lady shall have the kingdom."

The Prince went back to the White Cat, and told her what his father had said. She replied—

"Cut off my head and my tail."

At last he consented : instantly the Cat was transformed into a beautiful Princess ; for she had been condemned by a wicked fairy to appear as a Cat, till a young Prince should cut off her head and tail. The Prince and Princess went to the old King's court, and she was far more beautiful than the ladies brought by the other two Princes. But she did not want the kingdom, for she had four of her own already. One of these she gave to each of the elder brothers of the young Prince, and over the other two she ruled with her husband, for the young Prince married her, and they lived happily together all their lives.

In Mr. Morley's *Fairy Tales*, there is a funny passage :—" 'I wonder,' said a sparrow, 'what the eagles are about, that they don't fly away with the Cats? And now I think of it, a civil question cannot give offence.' So the sparrow finished her breakfast, went to the eagle, and said :—

" ' May it please your royalty, I see you and your race fly away with the birds and the lambs that do no harm. But there is not a creature so malignant as a Cat ; she prowls about our nests, eats up our young, and bites off our own heads. She feeds so daintily that she must be herself good eating. She is lighter to carry than a bird, and you would get a famous grip in her loose fur. Why do you not feed upon Cat ?'

" ' Ah !' said the eagle, 'there is sense in your question. I had the worms to hear this morning, asking me why I did not breakfast upon sparrows. Do I see a morsel of worm's skin on your beak, my child ?'

" The sparrow cleaned his bill upon his bosom,

and said :—' I should like to see the worm who came with that enquiry.'

" ' Come forward, worm,' the eagle said. But when the worm appeared, the sparrow snapped him up, and ate him. Then he went on with his argument against the Cats."

Everybody has heard of the Kilkenny Cats, and how they fought in a saw-pit with such ferocious determination, that when the battle was over, nothing was remaining of either combatant except his tail. Of course, we none of us suppose that the tale is true, but some writers think that the account of the mutual destruction of the contending Cats was an allegory designed to typify the utter ruin to which centuries of litigation and embroilment on the subject of conflicting rights and privileges tended to reduce the respective exchequers of the rival municipal bodies of Kilkenny and Irishtown—separate corporations existing within the liberties of one city, and the boundaries of the respective jurisdiction of which had never been marked out or defined by an authority to which either was willing to bow. The desperate struggles for supremacy of these parish worthies began A.D. 1377, and they fought, as only vestrymen can fight, a little over three hundred years, by the end of which time there was, as you may suppose, very little left of them but their tails, for, of course, there was a disinterested third person to whom the affairs were referred for arbitration, in the old way that the Cats appealed to the monkey upon the great cheese question—who swallowed his huge mouthful. In the end it would appear that all the property of either side was mortgaged, and bye-laws were passed by each party that their respective officers should be content with the dignity of their station, and forego all hope of salary till the suit at law with the other "pretended corporation" should be terminated.

Let this be as it may, one thing is certain : Kilkenny Cats are quite as amiable now-a-days as the Cats of any other city in Great Britain.

But there is another story of a great Cat fight in the same neighbourhood. One night in the summer time, all the Cats in the city and county of Kilkenny were absent from their homes, and next morning a plain near the city was strewn with thousands of slain Cats ; and it was reported that almost all the Cats in Ireland had joined in the fight, as was shown by the collars of some of the dead bearing the names of places in all quarters of the island. The cause of the quarrel is not stated, but there are yet men alive who knew persons since dead, who actually inspected the field—at least so they say.

Time out of mind the Cat has figured largely in our nursery annals—from the days of *Heigh Diddle-Diddle* and the *House that Jack Built* to the present moment. There is some waggishness, by the way, in Mr. Blanchard's version of the second mentioned rhyme, printed, as a sort of argument, in the book of the Drury Lane Pantomime :—

> " Anon, with velvet foot and Tarquin strides,
> Subtle Grimalkin to his quarry glides ;
> Grimalkin grim, that slew the fierce Rodent,
> Whose tooth insidious Johann's sackcloth rent.
> Lo ! how the deep-mouthed canine foe's assault,
> That vest th' avenger of the stolen malt
> Stored in the hallowed precincts of that hall
> That rose complete at Jack's creative call.
> Here stalks th' impetuous cow with crumpled horn,
> Thereon th' exacerbating hound was torn,
> Who bayed the feline slaughter-beast that slew
> The rat predacious, whose keen fangs ran through
> The textile fibres that involved the grain
> That lay in Han's inviolate domain."

The Cat is one of the principal of the *dramatis personæ* in Mr. D'Arcy Thompson's droll *Nursery Nonsense ;* and some of the most ingenious pictures Charles Bennett ever drew are to be found in his *Nine Lives of a Cat.* There is some good fun for little folks in a small book called *Tales from Catland*, with some masterly pictures from the graceful pencil of Mr. Harrison Weir; and there is another work called *Cat and Dog*, which I would recommend to all young readers. Of some other children's books, in which Pussy takes a prominent part, it behoves not the writer of this volume to say very much, for obvious reasons. I may, however, remark, that though a great admirer of the feline race, the artist who illustrated the works in question and this, has very limited notions concerning the way in which a Cat should be drawn, and has found, after all his trouble, that under his hand Pussy transferred to wood is very wooden indeed. It is some consolation to that artist, however, to reflect that Hogarth's Cats are anything but good ones. By the way, I always wonder when I look at that picture of the "Actress's Dressing Room" in the barn, whether poor strollers were ever driven to such an expedient as that of cutting a Cat's tail for the blood, and if so, how was it used? In George Cruikshank's "Bottle," do you remember in the first scene how happily the Cat and Kittens are playing on the hearth, and how in the next the kitten has disappeared, and the Cat, a poor half-starved wretch, is sniffing wistfully at an empty plate upon the table ? The change in Pussy's fortune is a clever touch ; but of all Cat pictures, one of the same artist's illustrations to the Brothers Mayhew's *Greatest Plague of Life* is that to be remembered ; I mean the one called " The Cat did it," in the chapter about Mrs. Burgess's Tom. There are a score and more of wonderful Cat stories in the *Münchener Bilderbögen,* and in other German books ; and who of those who have seen them can forget Grandville's extraordinary animals, so like Cats, and yet so human. There were some pictures that Charles Bennett drew, showing the gradual change of a human face into that of a beast, in which it was astonishing to note how easy and with what a few lines the transformation could be effected.

I might make this book a great deal longer (and more wearisome, perhaps) if I gave even the briefest outline of all the stories I have come upon during my long search ; but I believe that those to be found in these pages are among the best extant.

CHAPTER XI.

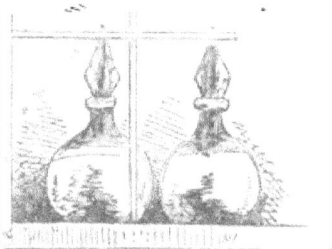

CHR

CHAPTER XI.

—o—

*Of Pussy Poorly, and of some
Curiosities of the Cats'-meat
Trade.*

—o—

" So sickly Cats neglect their
    fur attire,
  And sit and mope beside the
    kitchen fire."

Bombastes Furioso.

WRITER on Cats, when speaking of the
necessity of administering physic in certain cases, says that the bare thought
of so doing is sufficient to daunt at least
nine-tenths of the lady Cat-owners of the kingdom ;
and gives these directions to assist the timid fair one
in her arduous task :—

" Have ready a large cloth and wrap the patient therein, wisping the cloth round and round her body, so that every part of her, except the head, is well enveloped. Any one may then hold it between their knees, while you complete the operation. Put on a pair of stout gloves, and then with a firm hand open the animal's mouth wide !"

Poor Pussy ! From the formidable nature of these preparations, one would almost fancy that it was a full-grown tigress about to be doctored, and its iron mouth required a firm hand to wrench apart the jaws. To such inexperienced ladies as could require these directions, the writer's further advice not to pour down the Cat's throat too much at a time, comes very seasonably, but I am not too sure that Pussy will not be choked for all that. When properly managed, says he, "a sick Cat may be made to take pills or any other drug without risk of a severe scratching on your part, and danger of a dislocated neck on the part of suffering Grimalkin."

I can readily understand that there is small fear of the Cat's claws penetrating through five or six folds of stout calico, but about the safety of its neck I have my doubts. One, indeed, feels almost inclined to add, as a further safeguard for the trembling doctor, a suit of chain-mail or a diver's dress, such as the man wears who braves the dangers of the tank at the Polytechnic.

Seriously speaking, a lady who is kind to her domestic pets will have no trouble in giving them medicine. When they are Kittens, they should be taught to lie upon their backs, and in this attitude, with the head raised, the physic is easily enough administered. A sick Cat, too, does not fly from those for whom it has an affection; on the contrary, I have always known Cats to come for sympathy to those who nurse and feed them. Administer the physic with a teaspoon, if liquid, and be most careful when the dose has been given, to gently wash from the Cat's face or breast any drop of the stuff that may have fallen there, so that she may not find the nasty taste lingering about her when she goes to clean herself, as otherwise she has the unpleasantness of the physic long after the doses have been discontinued.

These are some of the complaints from which Cats suffer, and the best methods to be adopted for their cure :—

A cat is sometimes affected by a sort of distemper which attacks it between the first and third month of its life. The Cat or Kitten, when thus suffering, refuses its ood, seems to be sensitive

P

of cold, and creeps close to the fire or hides itself in any warm corner. A mild aperient—small doses of brimstone, for instance—should be administered. Whilst ill, feed the Cat upon light biscuit spread with butter. A little manna is a good thing if the Cat will eat it, and the animal should be kept warm and quiet. If, however, you see the sick Cat frequently vomiting, the vomit being a bright yellow frothy liquid, be very careful of the animal should she be a pet, for then the distemper is taking an ugly turn, and requires special attention. Probably before long the sickness will change to diarrhœa, which in the end will turn to dysentery if prompt measures be not taken. When the vomiting first comes on, give the Cat half a teaspoonful of common salt in about two teaspoonsful of water, as an emetic, for the purpose of clearing the stomach. Then to stop the sickness, give half a spoonful of melted beef marrow free from skin. If this is not found sufficient, the dose may be repeated.

Cats just reaching their full growth are liable to have fits. Male cats almost always have, at this time, a slight attack of delirium. When coming on, it may easily be known by an uneasy restlessness and a wildness of the eyes. In bad cases, the Cat, when seized with delirium, will rush about with staring eyes, sometimes fly at the window, but more often fly from your presence and hide itself in the darkest place it can find. If it have a regular fit, with frothing at the mouth, quivering limbs, etc., as in a human being so attacked, Lady Cust recommends that one of the ears be slightly slit with a sharp pair of scissors in the thin part of the ear. You must then have some warm water ready and hold the ear in it, gently rubbing and encouraging the blood to flow, a few drops even will afford relief. During the attack, the Cat does not feel, nor does it resist in the least, therefore the most timid lady might perform this little operation without fear. But where the symptoms are not so violent, a gentle aperient may do all that is required. A good alterative for them is half a teaspoonful of common salt in two teaspoonfuls of water, as mentioned above, though in this case it will not cause vomiting. Female Cats, Lady Cust says, are less subject to fits of delirium, and never have them after they have once nursed young ones, unless frightened into them, which all Cats easily are. In this, however, I think she is mistaken, for I have had a Cat so affected when nursing her second litter of Kittens. Another Cat of mine was seized with delirium, rushed suddenly out of the kitchen, and disappeared mysteriously for three days.

At the end of that time, the servant going to light the fire under the copper, the animal crawled forth from the copper hole very thin and weak, but otherwise seemingly cured of its strange complaint. All cats are subject to diarrhœa, and the signs of their so suffering are to be found in dull eyes, staring coat and neglected toilet, and the animal is very likely to die of the complaint unless the proper remedies be applied. As soon as it is discovered, give the Cat some luke warm new milk, with a piece of fresh mutton suet (the suet the size of a walnut to a teacupful of milk) melted, and mixed in it. If the patient be too ill to lap, administer the mixture a teaspoonful every two hours. Take care not to give it too much so as to make it sick. If there is no bile, you should give the Cat (full grown) a grain and a half of the grey powder used in such cases. If the diarrhœa still continue, Lady Cust suggests that a teaspoonful of the chalk mixture used by human beings, be tried, with seven or eight drops of tincture of rhubarb, and four or five of laudanum, every few hours until the complaint ceases. Cats will continue ill, her Ladyship says, for a few days, their eyes even fixed, but still with watching and care they may be cured. A teaspoonful at a time of pure meat gravy should be given now and then, but not until nearly two hours after medicine, to keep up the strength, until appetite returns.

There is a disease resembling the chicken-pox, which appears in the shape of eruptions upon a Cat's head and throat. It is, in these cases, advisable to rub the bad places with flour of brimstone mixed with fresh hog's lard, without salt. The Cat will lick some of this ointment off, and swallow it, which operation will assist the cure. Much of the necessity for physic is, however, avoided when the Cat is able to get some grass to eat, without which, I believe, it can never be in good health. I have a Tom Cat, which seems to be particularly partial to ribbon grass, but this, I should say, is quite an epicurean taste of his. According to Lady Cust, who is the greatest, indeed, the only authority on such matters, the hair swallowed by the Cat in licking itself, and conveyed into the stomach and intestines, where it remains in balls or long rolls, causing dulness and loss of appetite, is digested easily by adhering to the long grass; or if the mass is too large, as is often the case in the moulting season, especially with Angora Cats, it will be seen thrown up: long rolls of hair with grass; perfectly exclusive of any other substance. But, again, the Cat itself seems to know that grass is very needful

for the preservation of its health. The food and
prey it eats often disorder the stomach. On such
occasions, it eats a little grass, which, however, goes
no further than the commencement of the œso-
phagus ; this is irritated by the jagged and saw-
like margins of the blades of grass, and this
irritation is, by a reflex action, communicated to
the stomach, which, by a spasmodic action, rejects
its vitiated secretion.

It is very cruel and injurious to the mother to
destroy the whole litter of kittens at once, unless it
has some feline friend or relation to relieve it of its
milk : one of its grown-up children, or its husband,
will generally do so, without much persuasion. If
deprived of this resource, however, the frequent destruction of the kittens will, in all probability, cause
cancers, and in the end kill the Cat. If the mother
die, and the kittens be left orphans, they may be
easily reared by hand. Feed them with new milk,
sweetened with brown sugar—plain milk is too
astringent. To imitate the Cat's lick, wipe the
kittens with a nearly dry sponge, and soap and
water. A good way to feed them is to use a well-
saturated fine sponge, which the kittens will suck.
The most common way, however, is to pour the
milk gently down the throat from a pointed spoon.

I knew a lady who fed a pet kitten from her mouth, and it grew up extraordinarily affectionate and sagacious. But I have seen many cases where a Cat has conceived a strong affection towards a person who has never fed it, and scarcely ever noticed it.

I lately heard, on good authority, of a case of a lady, one of whose Cats came every morning to her bed-room door, at six o'clock precisely, making so much noise mewing, that it would awaken every one in the house, if she did not hasten to get up, open the door, and shake hands with it, after which ceremony it went quietly away. But, as a rule, these animals do not tax their masters' good nature to such an extent : a pat on the head now and then, a kind word now and again, nothing more is required.

Mr. Kingston says :—" I was calling on a delightful and most clever kind old lady, who showed me a very beautiful Tabby Cat, coiled up on a chair before the fire.

" ' Seventeen years ago,' said she, ' that Cat's mother had a litter : they were all ordered to be drowned, with the exception of one ; the servant brought me that one ; it was a tortoiseshell. ' No,' I said, ' that will always be looking dirty ; I will choose another ;' so I put my hand into the basket, and drew forth this tabby. The tabby has stuck by me ever since. When she came to have a family, she disappeared, but the rain did not, for it came pouring down through the ceiling, and it was discovered that Dame Tabby had made a lying-in hospital for herself in the thatched roof of our house. The damage she did cost us several pounds ; so we asked a bachelor friend, who had a good cook, fond of Cats, to take care of tabby the next time she gave signs of having a family, as we knew that she would be well fed. We sent her in a basket, well covered up, and she was carefully shut into a room, where she soon was able to exhibit a progeny of young mewlings. More than the usual number were allowed to survive ; and it was thought that she would remain quietly where she was ; but, at the first opportunity, she made her escape, and down she came all the length of the village ; and I heard her mewing at my bed-room door, early in the morning, to be let in. When I had stroked her back, and spoken kindly to her, off she went to look after her nurselings. From that day, every morning down she came regularly to see me, and would not go away till she had been spoken to and caressed. Having satisfied herself that I was alive and well, back she would go again. She never failed to pay me that one visit in the morning, and never came twice in the day, till she had weaned her kittens, and then every day she came back, and nothing would induce her to go away again : I had not the heart to force her back. From that day to this she has always slept at the door of my room.' Never was there more evident affection exhibited in the feline race."

With respect to a Cat's food, I think it should not have too much meat ; and I should prefer feeding it on scraps that have come from the table, to buying Cats' meat. If their taste be consulted upon the subject, almost all Cats are passionately fond of lights, particularly as they grow old ; and one elderly red-haired gentleman in particular, with whom I had once the honour of being acquainted, was in the habit of watching the pot whilst the lights boiled, with lively interest, sniffing the steam when the saucepan-lid was raised, and licking his lips in anticipation of joys to come, when he could gorge himself to his heart's content. As he was a very old gentleman, and enjoyed the privileges of age, he had unlimited lights supplied to him ; and it was his habit to eat as much as he could possibly swallow, and then lie down within sight of the plate, and catch uneasy snatches of sleep, waiting until he could go on again with his orgie, but racked meanwhile by horrid fears lest anyone else should get at his food, and only dozing off, as the saying is, one eye at a time. This same red Cat one day, when the servants were out, and I was alone in the garden, came to me mewing in a strange sort of way, looking, as I thought, very anxious, and running backwards and forwards between me and the house. At last, following him as he seemed to wish me to do, I accompanied him to the street-door, where I found the butcher's boy waiting with the lights.

In giving a Cat the scrapings of dirty plates, it is as well, if you value the animal's life, to remove the fish bones, should there be any among the leavings. Very frequently, as most Cats bolt their food, they get a bone sticking in their mouth or throat, of which they are unable to relieve themselves, and suffer much pain without their owner's guessing at the cause of their discomforture. A lady in a house I was staying at, had a Cat that got what was afterwards supposed to be a fish bone sticking in its mouth, far at the back, in such a way that it was unable to close its jaws. For two or three days it remained in this state, refusing all food, and looking in a woeful plight ; indeed, we afterwards supposed that it could not even lap ; but at the time, although we made several examinations of the sufferer, we could not discover what ailed it. At last, some one suggested seeking the aid of a veterinary surgeon, whose dignity seemed just a little bit ruffled by being called in for a Cat, and who, when he did come, did not bring his instruments with him. Nevertheless, he found out what was wrong, and forcing open the Cat's jaws, put in his finger to loosen what he called a fish-bone. Being rather fearful of getting a bite, he was somewhat hasty, and the bone jerked out, flew into the air, as he released his hold of the Cat's head, whereupon the Cat caught the bone as it fell, and instantly swallowed it, leaving us until this day in the dark as to the size and nature of the bone, and indeed, rather doubtful whether it was a bone at all.

In cases where the Cat is accidentally crippled, or should be so ill that it were better to put it out of its misery at once, the best plan is to send for a chemist, who for a small sum would administer the poison upon your own premises. I have known cases where men servants entrusted to take the animal to the chemist's shop, have thrown it down in the street, or killed it with unnecessary torture themselves, and pocketed the money they should have paid for the poisoning.

To administer the poison yourself is by no means a wise course, as probably you may give too much or too little, and in either case defeat your object. I know for a fact, that two medical students once barbarously practising experiments with poison on an unhappy Cat, twice poisoned the animal, as they supposed, and once actually buried it, of course not very deeply, after which it recovered again, and crawled into the house, rather to their alarm, as you may suppose, as on the second occasion it happened in the dead of night.

Those unable to procure the assistance of a doctor or chemist, can easily drown a Cat by putting it into a pail of water, and pressing another pail down upon it, care being taken of course to handle the Cat gently, so as not to alarm it before the last moment.

Concerning the Cats'-meat trade, Mr. Henry Mayhew gives many curious particulars, of which the following are some of the most amusing :—

" The Cats'-meat carriers frequently sell as much as ten pennyworth to one person, and there has been a customer to the extent of sixteen pennyworth. This person, a black woman, used to get out on the roof of the house, and throw it to the Cats on the tiles, by which conduct she brought so many stray Cats round about the neighbourhood, that the parties in the vicinity complained of the nuisance. The noise of about a hundred strange Cats, a little before feeding-time, about ten in the morning, was tremendous ; and when the meat was thrown to them, the fighting and confusion was beyond description.

" There was also a woman in Islington who used to have fourteen pounds of meat a-day. The person who supplied her was often paid two and three pounds at a time. She had often as many as thirty Cats at a time. Every stray Cat that came she would take in and support.

" The carriers give a great deal of credit ; indeed, they take but little ready money. On some days they do not come home with more than 2s. One with a middling walk, pays for his meat 7s. 6d. per day ; for this he has half-a-hundred weight : this produces him as much as 11s. 6d., so that his profit is 4s., which, I am assured, is about a fair average of the earnings of the trade. One carrier is said to have amassed £1,000 at the business : he usually sold from 1½ to 2 cwt. every morning, so that his profits were generally from 16s. to £1 per day. But the trade is much worse now : there are so many at it, they say, that there is barely a living for any."

A carrier assured Mr. Mayhew he seldom went less than thirty, and frequently forty miles, through the streets every day. The best districts are among the houses of tradesmen, mechanics, and labourers. The coachmen in the mews at the back of the squares are very good customers.

" ' The work lays thicker there,' said one carrier. 'Old maids are bad, though very plentiful customers : they cheapen the carriers down so that they can scarcely live at the business : they will pay one half-penny, and owe another, and forget that after a day or two.' The Cats'-meat dealers generally complain of their losses from bad debts : their customers require credit frequently to the extent of £1.

" 'One party owes me 15s. now,' said a carrier, 'and many 10s. ; in fact, very few people pay ready money for the meat.'

" The best days for the Cats'-meat business are Mondays, Tuesdays, and Saturdays. A double quantity of meat is sold on the Saturday ; and on that day and Monday and Tuesday, the weekly customers generally pay."

" The supply of food for Cats and Dogs is far greater than may be generally thought.

" 'Why, sir,' said one of the dealers, ' can you tell me how many people's in London?' On Mr. Mayhew's replying, upwards of two millions; 'I don't know nothing whatever,' said the man, 'about millions, but I think there's a Cat to every ten people, aye, and more than that; and so, sir, you can reckon.'"

Mr. Mayhew told him this gave a total of 200,000 Cats in London, but the number of inhabited houses in the Metropolis was 100,000 more than this, and though there was not a Cat to every house, still, as many lodgers as well as householders kept Cats, he added, "that he thought the total number of Cats in London might be taken at the same number as the inhabited houses, or 300,000 in all."

" 'There is not near half so many Dogs as Cats; I must know, for they all knows me, and I serves about 200 Cats and 70 dogs. Mine's a middling trade, but some does far better. Some Cats has a hap'orth a day, some every other day; werry few can afford a penn'orth, but times is inferior. Dogs is better pay when you've a connection among' em.'

" A Cats'-meat carrier who supplied me with information," says the same writer, "was more comfortably situated than any of the poorer classes that I have yet seen. He lived in the front room

of a second floor, in an open and respectable quarter
of the town, and his lodgings were the perfection of
comfort and cleanliness in an humble sphere.   It
was late in the evening when I reached the house;
I found the 'carrier' and his family preparing the
supper.   In a large morocco leather easy chair sat
the Cats'-meat carrier himself; his blue apron and
black shiny hat had disappeared, and he wore a
'dress' coat and a black satin waistcoat instead.
His wife, who was a remarkably pretty woman, and
of very attractive manners, wore a 'Dolly Varden'
cap, placed jauntily on the back of her head, and
a drab merino dress.   The room was cosily car-
peted; and in one corner stood a mahogany
'crib,' with cane-work sides, in which one of the
children was asleep.   On the table was a clean white
table-cloth, and the room was savoury with the
steaks and mashed potatoes that were cooking on
the fire.   Indeed, I have never yet seen greater
comfort in the abodes of the poor.   The cleanliness
and wholesomeness of the apartment were the more
striking from the unpleasant associations connected
with the calling.

"It is believed by one who has been engaged at
the business for 25 years, that there are from 900 to
1,000 horses, averaging 2 cwt. of meat each, little

and big, boiled down every week; so that the quantity of cats' and dogs' meat used throughout London is about 200,000 lbs. per week, and this, sold at the rate of 2½d. per lb., gives £2,000 a-week for the money spent in cats' and dogs' meat, or upwards of £100,000 a-year, which is at the rate of £100 worth sold annually by each carrier. The profits of the carriers may be estimated at about £50 each per annum. The capital required to start in this business varies from £1 to £2. The stock-money needed is between 5*s*. and 10*s*. The barrow and basket, weights and scales, knife and steel, or blackstone, cost about £2 when new, and from 15*s*. to 4*s*. second hand.

Mr. Mayhew also states the London dogs' and cats' meat carriers to number at least one thousand. "The slaughtermen," he says, "are said to reap large fortunes very rapidly. Many of them retire after a few years and take large farms. One after twelve years' business retired with several thousand pounds, and has now three large farms. The carriers are men, women, and boys. Very few women do as well at it as the men. The carriers are generally sad drunkards. Out of five hundred it is said three hundred at least spend £1 a head a-week in drink. One party in the trade told me that he knew a carrier who would spend 10s. in liquor at one sitting. The profit the carriers make upon the meat is at present only a penny per pound. In the summer time the profit per pound is reduced to a halfpenny, owing to the meat being dearer, on account of its scarcity."

The following are, as well as I can remember, the words of an old song, to the tune of " Cherry Ripe," that were sung in some play :—

> " Cats'-meat, Cats'-meat—meat, I cry,
> On a skewer—come and buy ;
> From Hyde Park Corner to Wapping Wall,
> All the year I Cats'-meat bawl ;
> Cats'-meat, Cats'-meat—meat, I cry,
> On a skewer—come and buy."

CHAPTER XII.

CHAPTER XII

—o—

Of Wild Cats, Cat Charming,
etc.

—o—

ITHOUT entering into any very lengthened details, I will here make room for a few natural history notes, collected from various sources :—

The Cat belongs to the same family as the lion, tiger, panther, leopard, puma, serval, ocelot, and lynx. The tribe is, perhaps, one of the best defined in zoology, all its members having characteristics of structure and habit not to be confounded with those of other animals. The rounded head and pointed ears, the long, lithe body, covered with fine silky hair, and often beautifully marked; the silent, stealthy step, occasioned by treading only on the fleshy ball of the foot ; the sharp, retractile claws, the large, lustrous eyes, capable, from the expansive power of the pupil, of seeing in the dark ; the whiskered lip, the trenchant, carnivorous teeth, and the tongue covered with recurved, horny prickles, are common to all.

In their habits and manners of life they are equally akin : they inhabit the forest and the brake, sleeping away the greater part of their time, and only visiting the glade and open plain when pressed by hunger. They are for the most part nocturnal in their habits, being guided to their prey by their peculiar power of vision, by their scent, and by their hearing, which is superior to that of most other animals. Naturally, they are strictly carnivorous, not hunting down their prey by a protracted chase, like the wolf and dog, but by lying in wait, or by moving stealthily with their supple joints and cushioned feet till within spring of their victims, on which they dart with a growl, as if the muscular effort of the moment were painful even to themselves. Whether the attack be that of a tiger on a buffalo, or that of a Cat on a helpless mouse, the mode of action is the same—a bound with the whole body from the distance of many yards, a violent stroke with the fore foot, a clutch with the claws, which are thrust from their sheaths, and a half-tearing, half-sucking motion of the jaws, as if the animal gloated in ecstacy over the blood of its victim.

This mode of life has gained for these animals the common epithets of "cruel, savage, and bloodthirsty," and has caused them to be looked upon by the uninformed as monsters in creation. When its natural instincts shall die out, then also will the tiger cease to exist ; and were the whole world peopled and cultivated equally with our own island, the feline family would be limited to a single genus—namely, the humble Cat. But as things are at present constituted, the valleys and plains of the tropics are clothed with an extensive vegetation, supporting numerous herbivorous animals, which could only be kept within due limits by the existence of carnivora, such as the lion, tiger, leopard, and panther.

The distribution of the feline animals is governed by those conditions to which we have alluded ; and thus the puma inhabits the North American prairie ;

the jaguar the savannahs of South America; the lion the arid plains of Africa and Asia; the tiger and panther the tropical jungles of the old world ; the minor species, as the ocelot and lynx, have a wider range in both worlds, while the domestic Cat associates with man in almost every region. With the exception of the latter, none of the other genera have been tamed or domesticated, so that they are strictly "wild beasts," against which man wages a ceaseless war of extirpation. It is true that, in the East, one species of leopard is trained for hunting, but this only very sparingly, and even then he does not follow the game by scent, but is carried by the hunters, and only let loose when he is within a few bounds of the animal. It must not be inferred, however, that they are untameable, for every creature is capable, more or less, of being trained by man, provided it receives due attention ; and we have sufficient evidence in the wonderful feats performed by the lions and tigers of Mr. Carter and Van Amburgh, that the felinæ are by no means destitute of intelligent docility. The truth is, there is no inducement to tame them, and thus the Cat, the most diminutive of the family, and the only one of direct utility to civilise, is likely to continue, as it ever has been, the sole domesticated member.

The wild Cat is more plentiful in the wooded districts of Germany, Prussia, and Hungary than in any other part of Europe. It is found also in the north of Asia and in Nepaul. Besides the true wild Cat, there are other species of felis which, on account of their resemblance to the tiger, are called "Tiger-Cats": they are found in all parts of the world, with the exception of Europe. The largest of this family is the Rimau-Dahan, an inhabitant of Sumatra. When full grown, it measures over seven feet from the nose to the tip of its tail, which appendage, however, monopolises three feet six of the whole. It is nearly two feet high at the shoulders : its colour is light grey, striped and spotted with jet black. One of the first specimens of this Tiger-Cat seen in England was brought here by Sir Stamford Raffles, who procured two of them from the banks of the Bencoolen River.

" Both specimens," writes this gentlemen, " while in a state of confinement, were remarkable for good temper and playfulness ; no domestic kitten could be more so ; they were always courting intercourse with persons passing by, and in the expression of their countenance, which was always open and smiling, showed the greatest delight when noticed, throwing themselves on their backs, and delighting in being tickled and rubbed. On board the ship there was a small dog, who used to play round the cage and with the animals ; and it was amusing to observe the playfulness and tenderness with which the latter came in contact with their inferior sized companion. When fed with a fowl that died, they seized the prey, and after sucking the head, and tearing it a little, amused themselves for hours in throwing it about and jumping after it, in the manner that a Cat plays with a mouse before it is quite dead. This species of Cat never seems to look on man or children as his prey ; and the natives assert that, when wild, it lives chiefly on poultry, birds, and small deer."

The colour of the wild Cat is more uniform than that of the domestic species. On a ground colour of pale reddish-yellow are dark streaks extending over the body and limbs, forming pretty much the sort of pattern exhibited on the tiger's robe. From the back of the neck to the spine, a line of very dark spots extends to the tail, which is short and bushy, and has a black tip. The feet and insides of the legs are yellowish grey. In the female, which is smaller that the male, the colours are not as distinct. The medium size of a full-grown male wild Cat is as follows :—Length of head and body,

1 foot 10 inches ; length of head, 3½ inches ; length of ears, 2½ inches ; length of tail, 11 inches. The wild Cat affects rocky and densely-wooded districts, living in holes or in hollow trees. According to Mr. St. John, a wild Cat will sometimes take up its residence at no great distance from a house, and, entering the hen-houses and outbuildings, carry off fowls or even lambs, in the most audacious manner. Like other vermin, the wild Cat haunts the shores of lakes and rivers, and it is, therefore, easy to know where to lay a trap for it. Having caught and killed one of the colony, the rest of them are sure to be taken, if the body of their slain relative be left in some place not far from their usual hunting-ground, and surrounded with traps, as every wild Cat which passes within a considerable distance of the place will to a certainty come to it.

America has several Tiger-Cats, foremost amongst which may be mentioned the Ocelot. Two of these animals were kept at the Tower of London, at the time when that ancient fortress counted a menagerie among its other attractions ; and of one of these Mr. Bennett gives the following description :—

" Body when full grown nearly 3 feet in length ; tail rather more than 1 foot ; medium height about

18 inches. Ground colour of fur grey, mingled
with a slight tinge of fawn, elegantly marked with
numerous longitudinal bands, the dorsal one con-
tinuous and entirely black, the lateral (six or seven
on each side) consisting for the most part of a series
of elongated spots, with black margins, sometimes
completely distinct, sometimes running together.
The centre of each spot is of a deeper fawn than
the ground colour external to it ; this deeper tinge
is also conspicuous on the head and neck, and on
the outside of the limbs, all of which parts are
irregularly marked with full black lines and spots
of various sizes. From the top of the head, between the ears, there pass backwards towards the
shoulders, two or more, frequently four, uninter-
rupted diverging bands, which enclose a narrow
fawn-colour space, with a black margin ; between
these there is a single longitudinal, somewhat inter-
rupted, narrow black line, occupying the centre of
the neck above. Ears short and rounded, exter-
nally margined with black, surrounding a large
central whitish spot : under parts of the body
whitish, spotted with black, and the tail, which is
of the same ground colour with the body, also
covered with black spots. This animal is a native
of Mexico and Paraguay : its home is the gloomiest

depths of the forest, where all day long it lies
quiet, but, as night advances, comes out to prey
on birds and small quadrupeds. It is said to be a
particularly cunning creature, and sometimes, when
other stratagems to replenish his larder have failed,
to stretch himself all along the bough of a tree and
sham death. The monkeys of the neighbourhood
have no greater enemy than the Ocelot, therefore it
is only natural that, when they find him dead, they
would be much rejoiced, and call together their
friends and relations to see the pretty sight. The
treacherous ocelot is, however, meanwhile keeping
sharp watch through a tiny chink of his eyelids,
and when the rejoicing is at its highest, up he
jumps, and, before the monkey-revellers can recover
from their fright, at least a couple will feel the fatal
weight of his paw. There are several ocelots, the
painted, the grey, and the common, among others.
In captivity, few animals are more surly and spiteful, until they grow thoroughly well acquainted
with their keepers or others who court their notice.
There is, however, one weapon keener than the
sharpest sword, more potent than the Armstrong
gun, more powerful than all the gunpowder and
bullets ever made, and yet so simple, that the boy
yet in pinafores may direct it : to this weapon the

suspicious tiger-cat succumbs, and the name of this weapon is—*Kindness!* So armed, the Rev. J. G. Wood conquered a body of Ocelots exhibited at the menagerie. He says:—

"Several of these animals, when I first made their acquaintance, were rather crabbed in disposition, snarled at the sound of a strange step, growled angrily at my approach, and behaved altogether in a very unusual manner, in spite of many amicable overtures. After a while, I discovered that these creatures were continually and vainly attempting the capture of certain flies, which buzzed about the cage; so I captured a few large bluebottle flies, and poked them through a small aperture in the cage, so that the Ocelot's paw might not be able to reach my hand. At first the ocelots declined to make any advance in return for the gift, but they soon became bolder, and at last freely took the flies as fast as they were caught. The ice was now broken, and in a very short time we were excellent friends, the angry snarl being exchanged for a complacent composed demeanour. The climax to their change of character was reached by giving them a few leaves of grass, for which they were, as I thought they would be, more anxious than for the flies. They tore the green blades out of my hand, and

enjoyed the unaccustomed dainty undisturbed.
After this, they were quite at their ease, and came
to the front of the cage whenever I passed."

The Colocolo is another tiger-cat: it is an inhabitant of Guiana, and though not more than a
third the size of the Rimau-Dahan, is a most formidable enemy to the smaller animals of the forests
which it inhabits. It is related by Mr. Wood that
a specimen of this creature was shot on the banks
of a river, in Guiana, by an officer of rifles, who
stuffed it, and placed the skin to dry on the awning
of his boat. As the vessel dropped down the river,
it passed under overhanging boughs of large trees,
on which rested numerous monkeys. Generally
when a boat passed along a river, the monkeys,
which inhabit the trees that border its banks, displayed great curiosity, and ran along the boughs,
so as to obtain a close view of the strange visitant.
Before the Colocolo had been killed, the passage of
the boat had been attended, as usual, by the inqui-
sitive monkeys, but when the stuffed skin was exhibited on the awning, the monkeys were horribly
alarmed, and instead of approaching the vessel, as
they had before done, trooped off with prodigious
yells of terror and rage. From this universal fear
which the sight of the animal occasioned to the

monkeys, it may be conjectured that the Colocolo is in the habit of procuring its food at the expense of the monkey tribes. Of the tiger-cat in Africa, the Serval may be taken as the type : it is about two feet long, exclusive of the tail, which measures nine inches, and is a foot in height at the shoulders. Its upper parts are clear yellow, and its under parts white, and its entire body is spotted with black. Among the Dutch settlers it is known as " Bosch-katte," or " Bush-cat." It is an inoffensive creature, *not* easily irritated, and behaving generally like our own familiar grimalkin.

The wild Cat of Ireland would seem to be quite as savage a fellow as his Scotch cousin. In Maxwell's " *Wild Sports of the West,*" is a story of one of these animals, which was killed after a severe battle : it was of a dirty grey colour, double the size of the common house Cat, and with formidable teeth and claws. It was a female, and was tracked to its burrow under a rock, and caught with a rabbit-net. So flimsy an affair, however, was scorned by the fierce brute, which speedily rent a hole with its teeth and claws, and was about to run off, when the lad who had set the snare seized it by the neck. It was finally dispatched by a blow of an iron spade. The lad, however, was so terribly wounded as to necessitate his removal to an hospital, where he for some time remained, in peril of lock-jaw.

The following narrative is furnished by Mr. St. John :—

"Once, when grouse shooting, I came suddenly, in the rough and rocky part of the ground, upon a family of two old and three half-grown wild Cats. In the hanging birch-woods that bordered some of the highland streams and rocks, the wild Cat is still not uncommon ; and I have heard their wild and unearthly cries echo afar in the quiet night as they answer and call to each other. I do not know a more harsh and unpleasant cry than the cry of the wild Cat, or one more likely to be the origin of superstitious fears in the mind of an ignorant Highlander. These animals have great skill in finding their prey ; and the damage they do to the game must be very great, owing to the quantity of food which they require. When caught in a trap, they fly, without hesitation, at any person who approaches them, not waiting to be assailed. I have heard many stories of their attacking and severely wounding a man, when their retreat has been cut off. Indeed, a wild Cat once flew at me in a most determined manner. I was fishing in a river in

Sutherlandshire, and in passing from one pool to another, had to climb over some rocky and broken ground. In doing so, I sank through some rotten moss and heather up to my knees, almost upon a wild Cat, who was concealed under it. I was quite as much startled as the animal herself could be when I saw the wild looking beast rush out so unexpectedly from between my legs, with every hair on her body standing on end, making her look twice as large as she really was. I had three small sky-terriers with me, who immediately gave chase, and pursued her till she took refuge in a corner of a rock, where, perched in a kind of recess, out of reach of her enemies, she stood with her hair bristled out, and spitting and growling like a common Cat. Having no weapon with me, I laid down my rod, cut a good sized stick, and proceeded to dislodge her. As soon as I came within six or seven feet of the place, she sprang right at my face, over the dogs' heads. Had I not struck her in mid-air, as she leapt at me, I should probably have got some severe wound. As it was, she fell, with her back half broken, among the dogs, who, with my assistance, dispatched her. I never saw an animal fight so desperately, or one so difficult to kill. If a tame Cat has nine lives, a wild Cat must have a dozen."

That a long course of domestic drill is insufficient to win a Cat from its native savagery, is proved by the following scrap, lately culled from the *Swansea Herald*:—

"A fight of more than ordinary interest took place on the bank of the canal, near Kidwelly Quay, a few days ago. A domestic Cat, making her usual walk in search of prey along the embankment, was attacked by an otter of no small dimensions, and was in an instant tossed into the middle of the canal, and there had to fight, not for the 'belt,' but for her life, in an uncongenial element. But very soon they were observed by some sailors and shippers, employed not far from the scene of contest, who hastened to witness the strange occurrence. Either from fear of the men, or of its formidable antagonist, the otter relinquished its hold, and poor Puss safely landed, amidst hearty cheers and congratulations. But Puss, not being content with the laurels she had won in the first contest, went out again on the following day, and, strange to say, the old combatants met again, and the otter, with undiminished pluck, attacked the Cat on land. The contest became very severe, but ultimately the otter was glad to regain its watery refuge, and leave Puss the victor the second time, without suffering very considerably from an encounter with such a formidable foe."

A writer on the subject of wild cats says—

"When a domesticated creature is no longer found in the wild state anywhere, like the camel and the lama, or when a reasonable scepticism may be entertained respecting the species assumed to be its savage ancestor, as is the case with the dog and the fowl, the steps of all our reasonings march straight into a blind alley, from which there is no issue, except by turning back. I believe that there never was such an animal as a really wild Pussy. The supposition involves an absurdity. Whose legs could she rub in a state of nature? On whose arrival could she set up her back, and arch her tail, and daintily tread on the same little spot? From what carpet, Kidderminster or Brussels, could she gently pull the threads with her claws? In what dairy could she skim the cream? From what larder could she steal cold roast pheasant? And if she did not do these things, or some of them, would she be a genuine Puss? No, no! I believe that Adam and Eve had a nice little tortoiseshell to purr between them, as they sat chatting on a sunny bank, and that a choice pair of tabbies slumbered, with half-shut eyes, and their feet turned under them, before the fire, which was the centre of Noah's family circle on board the Ark!"

Apropos of Cat-charming or Cat-taming, here are two anecdotes from Mr. Beeton's book :—

" I have," says the writer, " a vivid recollection of once charming a Cat to within an inch of getting myself thoroughly well thrashed. There lived in our neighbourhood a kind-hearted old gentleman, who was good enough to take a fancy to my ungrateful self, and would frequently invite me (he was a bachelor) to dine with him. The dining part of the business I had not the least objection to ; but after dinner, when we had chatted till he fell into a doze, it became, to a boy nine years old, rather tedious. It was on one such occasion that I behaved so disgracefully. The old gentleman was nodding, with his slippered feet crossed lazily before the fire, and a fat tortoiseshell Cat, his property, lay along the rug, placidly asleep, too. Had I been a good boy, I should have sat still, and turned the leaves of Fox's *Book of Martyrs* till my friend awoke ; but I was not a good boy: I felt myself like a martyr, doomed to the dreadful torture of sitting still. I felt in my pocket for a top-string I had there, and for a minute or so amused myself by bobbing the button at the end of the string on to the nose of the tortoiseshell

Cat, till I had aroused that lazy animal to a state of extreme irritability. This sport, after a while, grew tame, so I shifted the string, and allowed it to dangle within an inch of my host's feet. Really, it was done with scarce a thought, but the result was rather astonishing. The Cat, who all the time kept her eye on the tormenting string, no sooner saw it at a distance convenient to spring at, than she made a bound, and, missing the cord, fiercely embraced one of the slippered members with ten of her talons. For the moment I was too frightened to weigh the possible consequences of laughing, and laughed outright, which, with the sudden bound the old gentleman gave, so alarmed the tortoiseshell Cat, that she flew towards the door like a mad Cat. I doubt, however, whether its utmost agility would have saved it from the tongs, with which its outraged master pursued it, had I not ashamedly explained the matter, and begged forgiveness."

" I have certainly, in my time, made the acquaintance of some queerish Cats. When quite a little boy, there was attached to our house, a quaint black and white Cat whose sole recommendation was that he was a magnificent mouser; nay, to such lengths would he carry his passion for hunting, as regularly to haunt a ditch that existed in the neighbourhood for the purpose of pursuing and capturing water-rats, which class of vermin he despatched in a manner that at once secured the death of the rat, and himself immunity from the rat's teeth. Seizing the animal by the back of the neck, the Cat, by a sudden wriggle, threw himself on his back, and at once transferred the custody of the rat from his mouth to his fore-paws, holding it neatly behind the shoulders, while with his hind talons he cruelly assailed the unlucky animal's loins and ribs till it ceased to struggle. I have stated that the Cat in question was attached to our house, and that certainly was the extent of his intimacy, for he was attached to nobody residing there. Myself, he particularly disliked, and although he never considered it beneath his dignity to steal any article of food from me, would never accept my overtures of friendship. I have reason to believe that his special dislike to me arose out of a pair of boots possessed by me at that period. They were creaking boots, and fastened with laces. Whether it was that their loud creaking as I moved about the room in them, reminded him of the squeak of rats, or whether, not being a particularly tidy boy, the before-mentioned laces were sometimes allowed to trail rats'-tail-wise, aggravatingly heightened the illusion, I can't say ; I only know that as sure as I happened to allow my small feet to swing loosely while seated at breakfast or dinner, so surely would the black and white Cat, if he were in the room, make a sudden dash at the hated boots, giving my leg a severe wrench in his endeavour to fling himself on his back for the purpose of tearing the life out of them after his own peculiar mode.

"My enemy was, however, finally subdued, and in a rather curious way. Some one brought me one of those difficult musical instruments known as a mouth organ, and delighted with my new possession, I was torturing it as I sat on a seat in the garden. Suddenly there appeared in a tree just above my head, my foe, the black and white Cat, with his tail waving from side to side, his eyes staring, and his mouth twitching in an odd sort of way. I must confess that I was rather alarmed, and in my nervous condition, I might be excused if I construed the expression of the Cat's countenance to intimate, " Here you are then with another hideous noise, a noise that is even more suggestive of rat squeaking than your abominable boots ; however, I've caught you by yourself this time, so look out for your eyes." I did not, however, cease playing my organ; my enemy's green eyes seemed to fascinate me, and my tremulous

breath continued to wail on the organ pipes. Slowly
the black and white Cat descended the tree, and
presently leapt at my feet with a bound that
thrilled through me, and expelled a scream-like
note from my instrument. But to my astonishment,
my enemy did not attack me ; on the contrary, he
approached the offending boots humbly, and caressed
them with his head. Still I continued to play, and
after every inch of my Bluchers had received
homage from the Cat's hitherto terrible muzzle,
he sprang on the seat beside me, and purred and
gently mewed, and finally crept on to my shoulders
and lovingly smelt at the mouth-organ as I played
it. From that day hostilities ceased between us.
He would sit on my shoulders for half an hour
together, and sing, after his fashion, while I played,
and I had only to strike up to lure him from any
part of the premises where he might happen to be.

" There used to come to our house a young man
who played the trombone, and having heard the
story, insisted that there was nothing in it,—that all
Cats like music, and that savage as was our Cat to
strangers, he would be bound to conquer him with
a single blast of his favorite instrument. Next
time he came armed with the terrible-looking
trombone, which our Cat no sooner saw than, (as I

had predicted, for I knew his nature better than anyone else could) he took a violent dislike to it. A blast on the trombone ; the effect was as he prognosticated instantaneous, though not perfectly satisfactory ; the brazen note was immediately responded to by one equally loud from our Cat, who appeared to regard it as a challenge to combat, and thickened his tail and bared his teeth accordingly, at the same time swearing and spitting dreadfully. I need not say that the trombone-player was discomfited, while my fame as a Cat-charmer was considerably augmented."

Poor Pussy ! her character is not often properly understood, as we read elsewhere :—

" One or two common errors about Cats may be noticed. Many persons will destroy them when anything is the matter with them, whereas, in many cases they would recover with a little care. Some think they do not drink much, which is a mistake. Water should always be placed within their reach. As to their want of attachment, there is no doubt that is generally owing to the neglect (if not worse treatment) they often experience. Every animal will ordinarily return kindness for kindness ; and, if persons will only try, they will not find Cats an exception. But to knock an animal about, or hardly ever to notice it, and to punish severely any fault it may commit, are not ways to attach it to you. The writer has heard of more than one instance in which, on its master's death, a favourite Cat has gone away and not been seen again. There is a great diversity of character in Cats, as, indeed, in all animals. As to the colour, this is not of such importance as the shape. She should be well rounded, compactly formed, with small ears and fur of fine texture. It sometimes happens that ordinary-looking Cats have some very good qualities. Cats are very much afraid of each other : two of them will often look at one another over a plate for a long time, neither venturing to move or to take anything. At other times they are great bullies. One will get close up to another, and scream into his ear until the other gradually shrinks back and runs off when he has got clear."

"The Chinese, it seems," says another writer, "learn the hour of the day by looking into the eyes of their Cats ; but I imagine that if Cats could speak Chinese, they would tell us, not only what o'clock it is, but also what is the day of the week. When a boy, I was a great pigeon-keeper : pigeon-keeping in a town leads to excursions on the roofs. Excursions over roofs lead sometimes to neck-breaking, sometimes to strange discoveries. Our neighbour at the back was a large coach-builder, and the nearest buildings were his forges. On week days, I beheld, during my airy rambles, nothing but the blacksmiths hammering away at bolt, and spring, and tire, and nail ; but on Sundays, except in case of inclement weather, the warm tiles that covered the forges were tenanted by numerous parties of Cats. There they sat, all day long, admiring one another, holding silent deliberations, determining in their minds which partner they should select for the evening's concert and ball. While daylight lasted, it was a Quaker's meeting, silent and sober ; but after dark—the darker the better—leaps and friskings were audible, with vocal effects of long-swelling notes, such as called forth Peter Pindar's Ode to the Jewish Cats of Israel Mendez, whose opening line is—

" Singers of Israel ! O, ye singers sweet !"

From Monday morning till Saturday night not a Cat was to be seen : they knew when Sunday came round, as well as I did, from the low temperature of the tiles.

It is very common for Cats to select one member of a family on whom they lavish all their fondness,

while towards the others they comport themselves
with the utmost indifference. " I remember," says a
lady, " there was a Cat with her Kittens found in a
hole in the wall, in the garden of the house where
my father-in-law lived. One of the kittens, being a
very beautiful black one, was brought into the
house, and almost immediately attached himself in
a very extraordinary way to me. I was in mourn-
ing at the time, and, perhaps, the similarity of the
hue of my dress to his sable fur, might first have
attracted him ; but, however this may have been,
whenever he came into the room, he constantly
jumped into my lap, and evinced his fondness by
purring and rubbing his head against me in a very
coaxing manner. He continued thus to distinguish
me during the rest of his life ; and though I went
with my father-in-law's family every winter to
Dublin, and every summer to the country, the
change of abode (to which Cats are supposed to be
averse) never troubled my favourite, provided he
could be with me. Frequently, when we have been
walking home, after spending the evening out, he
has come running down half the street to meet us,
testifying the greatest delight. On one occasion,
when I had an illness, which confined me for upwards of two months to my room, poor Lee Boo

deserted the parlour altogether, though he had been always patted and **caressed** by every one there. **He** would **sit** for hours mewing disconsolately **at** my door ; **and** when he could, he would steal in, jump upon the bed, testifying his joy at seeing **me** by loud purring and coaxing, and sometimes licking **my hand.** The very day I went down, he resumed **his regular** attendance in the parlour."

Another lady describes how her Cat awoke her in the middle of the **night.** It sat down **by** the **bed-side** and mewed, while **it rubbed** itself backwards and forwards against the bedposts. The lady had no idea what was the matter, but felt sure there was something, and lighting the **candle,** found a dead mouse quite close to her. Satisfied **that the** lady had examined its capture, **Puss took** it off, and after playing with it for an hour, ate it up, leaving, as usual, the tail and paws. In the country or in farmhouses, the Cat will never fail **to** bring home birds **and mice, and,** in Southern climes, lizards and even snakes. **She** does this, however, **very much in pro-** portion to the amount of **kindness bestowed** upon her at home, **and** if this be altogether lacking, **the prey is only** shown to other Cats living in the same house, or to her own young, if she happens **to have any ; often** indeed, she **brings her** trophy immediately and only to her young.

There was a gentleman who had a tortoiseshell Cat, which, though he never fed it, or paid much attention to it, formed an attachment for him equal to that of a dog. It knew his ring at the bells, and at whatever time he came home, it was rubbing against his legs long before the servant came, saw him into the sitting-room, and then walked off. It was a very active animal, and usually went bird-catching during the night; but when its master rose, which was generally early in the morning, the Cat was always ready to receive him at the door of his room, and accompany him in his morning walk in the garden, alternately skipping to the tops of the trees, and descending and gambolling about him. When he was in his study, it used to pay him several visits in the day, always short ones; but it never retired till he had recognized it. If rubbing against his legs had not the desired effect, it would mount the writing-table, nudge his shoulder, and if that would not do, pat him on the cheek; but the moment he had shaken it by the paw, and given it a pat or two on the head, it walked off. When he was indisposed, it paid him several visits every day, but continued in the room; and although it was fond of society generally, and also of its food; it never obtruded its company during meals. Its attachment was thus quite disinterested, and no pains whatever had been taken to train it."

Here is a curious anecdote, culled from another source :—

" I have at the present time about my house a Cat that came into my possession under rather singular circumstances. Before we knew her, we had a Cat that gave perfect satisfaction, was a good mouser, and an affectionate mother. In the rear of our house, there is a shed, commonly used as a wood store, and frequented, at least, once a day. It is by no means a secluded place, and the door, through a weakness in its hinges, is constantly ajar.

" One morning there was discovered in the shed, not only a strange Cat, but a strange Kitten, with its eyes open, plump, and about a fortnight old. The strange Cat made no attempt to stir when the maid entered, but lay suckling her baby, and looking up with an expression that said as plainly as Cat language could,—

" ' A persecuted Cat and her Kitten at your service ; don't drive us out, that's a good creature.'

" More singular still, before the person appealed to could consider the case, our own Cat peeped into the shed, and after deliberately walking up to the refugees, and giving them a kindly touch with her nose, walked back to the servant and commenced to rub against her, purring the while, as though to manifest her goodwill towards the strangers, and to recommend a favourable consideration of their case, so they were taken in.

"As soon, however, as the novelty of the affair wore off, it began to dawn on us that we did not require a 'house-full' of Cats, though for that matter the four lived happily together. Which should we get rid of ? The strange Cat's kitten was too big to drown and too little to send adrift ; our own 'Topsy' and her daughter must, of course, be retained, so there was nothing left but to send away the strange she-Cat. She was rather a good-looking Cat, and that, coupled with her known cleverness, gave us good ground for supposing that she would soon find another home. It appeared, however, that we did not give her credit for being nearly so clever as she was.

"It was arranged that she should be conveyed in a basket to a certain square, about a quarter-of-a-mile distant, and there left to seek her fortune. To the best of everybody's belief, this arrangement was carried out to the letter, therefore the amazement of the entire household may be easily

imagined when, on reference being made to the
Cat-cupboard, to see how Topsy and her two young
charges were getting on, to find no Topsy at all,—
only the strange Cat and the two Kittens. How
the cheat had been accomplished, it was impossible
to say. That Topsy was not the Cat placed in the
basket was vouched for by two witnesses—one of
them had held the basket-lid open while the other
pushed the animal in.

" Perhaps, in my own mind, I have little doubt
how the business was so mulled, but I know that
in certain quarters there exists a belief, either that
by some sort of witchery the strange Cat put on so
Topsical an appearance as to deceive her would-be
smugglers, or that, after she was basketed, she
managed to sneak out, and either by persuasion
or force induced the unlucky Topsy to take her
place.

" However it came about, the result is, that the
strange Cat alone reigns at our house, to the jealous
exclusion of all her species. No one, I believe, has
any particular affection for her, but that circumstance is not observed to prey on her mind or to
interfere with her appetite. She devours her rations
with the air of a Cat that is conscious that she has
earned them, and as though she is aware, and rather

gloried than otherwise, in the knowledge that she is regarded as a cunning and manœuvring beast, that first, by hypocritical representations, induced an honest Cat to obtain for her a situation, and afterwards ungratefully contrived to push out her benefactress and progeny, and install herself in their place."

From the *Autobiography of Miss Cornelia Knight*, Lady Companion to the Princess Charlotte of Wales, I take the following scrap :—

"An old woman, who died a few years ago, in Ireland, had a nephew, to whom she left by will all she possessed. She happened to have a favourite Cat, which never left her, and even remained by the corpse after her death. After the will was read, in the adjoining room, on opening the door the Cat sprang at the lawyer, seized him by the throat, and was with difficulty prevented from strangling him. This man died about eighteen months after this scene, and, on his death-bed, confessed that he had murdered his aunt to get possession of her money."

The oft-quoted lines by Gray should not be omitted from *The Book of Cats* :—

"ON THE DEATH OF A FAVOURITE CAT,

" *Drowned in a Tub of Gold Fishes.*

" 'Twas on a lofty vase's side,
  Where China's gayest art had dyed
    The azure flowers that blow,
  Demurest of the tabby kind,
  The pensive Selima reclined,
    Gazed on the lake below.

" Her conscious tail her joy declared—
  The fair round face, the snowy beard,
    The velvet of her paws,
  Her coat, that with the tortoise vies,
  Her ears of jet, and emerald eyes—
    She saw and purred applause.

" Still had she gazed, but 'midst the tide,
  Two angel forms were seen to glide,
    The genii of the stream ;
  Their scaly armour's Tyrian hue,
  Though richest purple to the view,
    Betrayed a golden gleam.

" The hapless nymph, with wonder saw,
  A whisker first, and then a claw ;
    With many an ardent wish
  She stretched in vain to reach the prize ;—
  What female heart can gold despise?
    What Cat 's averse to fish ?

" Presumptuous maid, with looks intent,
  Again she stretched, again she bent,
    Nor knew the gulf between ;

(Malignant Fate sat by and smiled)—
The slippery verge her feet beguiled,
　　She tumbled headlong in.

" Eight times emerging from the flood,
　She mewed to every watery god
　　Some speedy aid to send ;
　No dolphin came, no nereid stirred,
　No cruel Tom, no Susan heard,—
　　Favourite has no friend.

" From hence, ye beauties, undeceived,
　Know one false step is ne'er retrieved,
　　And be with caution bold—
　Not all that tempts your wandering eyes
　And heedless hearts is lawful prize—
　　Not all that glitters gold."

These verses are well known, but those which
follow are less often met with : they are attributed
to George Tuberville, and written somewhere
about the beginning of the sixteenth century :—

"THE LOUER,

Whose mistresse feared a mouse, declareth that he would become a Cat
if he might haue his desire.

———

" If I might alter kind,
　　What, think you, I would bee ?
　Not Fish, nor Foule, nor Fle, nor Frog,
　　Nor Squirril on the Tree ;

The Fish the Hooke, the Foule
The lymed Twig doth catch,
The Fle the Finger, and the Frog
The Bustard doth dispatch.

" The Squirrill thinking nought,
That feately cracks the Nut ;
The greedie Goshawke wanting pray,
In dread of Death doth put ;
But scorning all these kindes,
I would become a Cat,
To combat with the creeping Mouse,
And scratch the screeking Rat.

" I would be present, aye,
And at my Ladie's call,
To gard her from the fearfull mouse,
In Parlour and in Hall ;
In Kitchen, for his Lyfe,
He should not shew his hed ;
The Peare in Poke should lie untoucht
When shee were gone to Bed.

" The Mouse should stand in Feare,
So should the squeaking Rat ;
All this would I doe if I were
Converted to a Cat."

But I think George must have been very far gone
when he wrote that piece of poetry, for I should
think that, even with the advantage of nine lives to
lose, a Cat's existence is rather too hazardous ;
and, by the way, that reminds me of some instances

where Pussy's natural prey have turned upon her in a most unpleasant manner ; thus :—

A Cat was observed on the top of a paled fence, endeavouring to get at a blackbird's nest, which was near it. The hen left the nest at her approach, and flew to meet her in a state of alarm, and uttered a wild cry. The cock bird, on perceiving the danger, showed signs of distress by sometimes settling on the fence just before the Cat, who was unable to make a spring in consequence of the narrowness of her footing. After a little while, the cock bird flew at the Cat, settled on her back, and pecked her head with so much violence that she fell to the ground, followed by the blackbird, who succeeded in driving her away. A second time the same scene occurred ; the blackbird was again victorious ; and the Cat became so intimidated at the attacks made upon her, that she gave over the attempts to get at the young ones. After each battle, the blackbird celebrated his victory with a song, and for several days afterwards he would hunt the Cat about the garden whenever she left the house. There is also an instance of a pair of blackbirds following a boy into a house, and pecking at his head, while he was conveying one of their young into it.

Here is another case :—

A lady who kept a tame Jack Hare, in giving an account of it, says, that if a Cat approached him he would sit upright, "square himself," as it were, and rub his paws together like a pugilist preparing for an encounter. With one stroke of his soft but strong paws, the hare would tear a strip of the hair, and often even the skin, from the Cat's back ; at other times he would make his sharp-cutting teeth meet in her neck ; and so formidable at last was the "timid hare" to the little "domestic tiger," that no sooner did Pussy spy her conqueror than she would fly in terror from his presence.

In these two anecdotes, as in many others, Pussy is exhibited in a very unamiable light ; but I hope that a few of the good traits I have been able to relate in the foregoing pages may weigh the balance in her favour with those inclined to judge her fairly. As a cruel destroyer of smaller and weaker animals she is most often painted, and so identified is she with that character, that it is difficult to make those personally unacquainted with her many good qualities to believe that any exist. In this way an actor, famous for his villains, becomes so very villainous, that even in a virtuous character we suspect him of hypocrisy, and expect that presently he will throw off the mask and assume his proper colours. By the way of allusion to a Cat on the stage, I think I can quote one of the most effective pieces that have been spoken.

Do any of my readers remember Robson acting in the burlesque of Medea? Upon the night of its production Ristori went to the Olympic to see his travestie of her great character. One of the finest passages in the tragedy is that in which Medea describes how like a tigress she will spring upon her intended victim. In Robert Brough's version the tigress is turned into a Cat, and Robson, with one of his intensely passionate bursts, used words, as well as I can recollect (I have not got a book by me), something after this fashion :—

> " How will I, eh ? The way the Cat jumps
> Upon a simple unsuspecting mouse
> Loose in the pantry,—no one in the house,—
> Nibbling away, with confidence unshaken,
> Eating his cheese up first to save his bacon.
> She's in no hurry. With dilating eyes,
> And undulating tail, she crouching lies,
> Till his enjoyments crises he is at,
> Then pounce ! she makes a spring, and has him—pat.
> To a short game of pitch and toss she treats him—
> Tears him to pieces slowly—SCRUNCH—then eats him."

While upon the subject of the theatre, I might add that it is a rule behind the scenes—a rule, however, very seldom enforced, if I am properly informed—that a Cat which crosses the scene when the curtain is raised shall be put to death.   Such an unappropriate appearance has, before now, spoilt the finest tragedy.   I think there is a story by Colonel Addison bearing upon an incident of this kind.

The Old Catch :—

> " When a good housewife sees a rat
>   In a trap in the morning taken,
>   With pleasure her heart goes pitte-pitte-pat,
>   For revenge of loss of bacon;
>   Then she throws it to the Dog or Cat,
>   To be worried, eat, or shaken,"

tolerably well indicates the popular notion of a Cat's duties, and the idea of keeping one for a pet, as birds are kept, would be thought by many a monstrous absurdity.   By the way, it is said that the best way to get rid of English rats is not to get a Dog or Cat to kill them, but to purchase two or three Australian rats, and let them loose among them.   They are to be purchased in London, and realise a high price from those who have faith in their frightening propensities, which I confess I have not.

With respect to Pussy's mouse-catching qualities, etc., a writer in a periodical says :—

" Most persons have heard of the beautiful contrivance by which the claws of these animals are preserved constantly sharp ; being drawn, when not used, by certain tendons, within a sheath or integument, while only the soft parts of the foot come in contact with the ground, thus enabling the animal to tread noiselessly. The roughness of the Cat's tongue is due to a multitude of horny papillæ (much stronger, of course, in lions and tigers), by which it is materially helped to keep itself clean,— a most important point, for cleanliness is a necessity to Cats, inasmuch, as if they had the slightest smell about them, their prey would detect their presence, and never come within their reach. As it is, the Cat is so free from smell that she may sit close to the holes of mice without their being aware of it, although they possess a fine sense of smell. A Cat never eats a morsel of anything, whatever it is, without afterwards sitting down to clean and wipe its face and lips. The caution for which it is so remarkable is likewise evinced in its choice of secluded spots for bringing up its offspring ; very often some hole or corner little thought of by the inmates of the house. If the young be removed and placed elsewhere, the mother will frequently take them again and again to the place chosen by herself. Another characteristic of the domestic Cat is an instinctive knowledge of the presence of danger. Even a chimney on fire, or the presence of strange workmen in the house, will make it very restless and uneasy, and on such occasions it will sometimes not go to rest even during the night. Every animal is endowed with peculiar means of self-defence; and as the Cat cannot trust, like the hare, to speed, on the approach of danger, it watches its enemy, occasionally taking side glances, or looking round for a place of refuge. On these occasions, notwithstanding its natural nervousness, it maintains great coolness. If a hole or shelter be near, it waits for an opportunity, or until its enemy looks away, and then rushes under cover, or runs up a tree or a wall, and immediately sits down and watches its enemy. If driven to an actual encounter, the smallness of its mouth and jaws preclude the use of its teeth to any great extent, but it can inflict considerable injury and acute pain with its sharp claws, which, perhaps, no dog, except a bulldog, can bear; indeed, few dogs like to attack a Cat at bay, though they all run after them. It is curious, too, that once in a place of safety, it never seeks to leave it, or loses sight of its enemy. A Cat on the safe side of an area railing will sit down and coolly watch a dog barking furiously at it.

"Its care and solicitude for its offspring are excessive and touching. If attacked while rearing them, it will not run away, but stand and defend them against any odds ; like the hare in similar circumstances, the Cat evinces immense power and courage, no matter how formidable the enemy may be. Of course the females of all animals possess more or less of this quality."

Cats have a much better time of it in France than here. A year or two since, the budget of the Imperial Printing Office in France, amongst other items, contained one for Cats, which caused some merriment in the Legislative Chamber during its discussion. According to the *Pays*, these Cats are kept for the purpose of destroying the numerous rats and mice which infest the premises, and cause considerable damage to the large stock of paper which is always kept there. This feline staff is fed twice a day, and a man is employed to look after them, so that for Cats'-meat and the keeper's salary no little expense is annually incurred, sufficient, in fact, to form a special item in the national expenditure. Of these animals a somewhat interesting anecdote is related. It appears that near to the Imperial Printing Office is situated the office of the Director of the Archives, and the gardens of the two establishments are adjacent. In that belonging to the latter gentleman, were kept a number of choice aquatic birds, for whose convenience a small artificial river had been constructed. Their owner suddenly discovered, one day, that his favourites were diminishing in a mysterious manner, and set a watch to ascertain the reason. Soon it was discovered who were the marauders—the Cats! The enraged director, acting in the spirit of the law, thought he had a perfect right to shoot and otherwise destroy these feline burglars, whenever he found them on his grounds, and accordingly did so. Traps were set, and soon half-a-dozen Cats paid the penalty of their crimes. The keeper of the Cats, also, by this time, found that the muster at meal-times was much scantier than usual, and reported to his superior, the director of the printing office. At first the workmen were suspected of killing them; but the appearance, one day, of a Cat with a broken snare round its neck,

put the keeper on a fresh scent, and ultimately led
to the discovery of the truth. The director thereupon complained to his brother official, who only
replied by pointing to the thinly-tenanted pond,
and saying that he would not have his birds destroyed if he could help it. The result was that a
fierce hostility reigned between the two establishments, until an arrangement was made by their
respective heads. By this treaty it was stipulated
that the Director of the Imperial Printing Office
should, on his part, cause every outlet by which
the Cats gained access to the gardens of the
Director of the Archives to be carefully closed, and
every means taken to prevent such a contingency ;
while, on the other hand, Monsieur, the Director of
the Archives, agreed never to molest any Cat
belonging to the Imperial Printing Office, who
should, by some unforeseen accident, obtain ad-
mittance into his garden. And thus, by this
famous treaty, the horrors of civil war were
averted !

Perhaps as curious an instance as any on record,
where Puss's powers as a watchman have been
called into requisition, may be found in a fact just
communicated to me. There is, it appears, a
family now residing near Richmond, who have a

black Cat nicknamed Snow Ball, which, during sowing time, every morning, punctually and dutifully presents himself to his owners, for the purpose of being fastened up by a cord, near the spot where the peas or other seed may have been newly sown ; and whilst thus keeping guard, woe betide any bird that might attempt to commit a depredation within Puss's reach.

CHAPTER XIII.

CHAPTER XIII.

—— o ——

ENTION has already been made of a
Cat concert in Paris, but we should not
forget that we once had an English actor
of the name of Harris, who took part in
the entertainments given by Foote at "the little
Theatre," who was called Cat Harris, in consequence of the talent he displayed in imitating the
mewing of the feline race. He burlesqued scenes
from Italian operas, and probably at that time the
squalling of a Cat was thought to be a very severe
satire on the foreign singers. Only a year or two
ago, however, I remember a music hall singer,
since dead, who sang a song called the *Monkey and*

the Nuts,—he being dressed something like a monkey;—with a peculiarly comic mewing and jabbering chorus. The since popular *Perfect Cure* is the air of this song, slightly altered, in the same way that the *Whole Hog or none* is altered from *Love's young Dream.*

The imitations of the singer I allude to (I think his name was McGown) were very good, and there was no occasion for him to tell you which was meant for the monkey and which the Cat, by no means superfluous information sometimes, when a young gentleman gives his notion of the voices of popular actors. By the way, do any of my readers remember the great Von Joel's celebrated " plack purd " and " trush," and how hard it was, occasionally, to tell which was " te trush " or which was " te plack purd "?

In talking of a Cat's fondness for fish (see page 73), I might also have mentioned the great liking these animals seem to have for the ends of asparagus, which I have often observed them devour with great eagerness.

Talking of fish-catching, an officer on board an Australian packet tells me that he has seen a Cat watch for hours on a windy night for flying fish, which jump on board if they see a light. From the same source I have learnt some curious facts relating to Puss at sea. "There are," he says, "generally two kinds of rats on board a ship, one kind going out, another coming home. While we were in the East India Docks, the rat-catcher caught twenty-five rats in his traps on board our ship, which we purchased and let loose in a malt bin extending the width of the ship. A Cat which we put among them killed all the brown rats, but did not touch the black ones, of which there were three. When she came in contact with a black rat she drew back, and made no attempt to harm it, although the black rats were much the smallest. Our ship, coming home from Sydney, was swarming with black rats, but I never knew a Cat to kill one, or even go near it. The reason of this I cannot explain.

"I have seen a Cat imitate a monkey in climbing up a loose-hanging rope. Of course it took a longer time to do it, but it did do it in the end."

Aboard ship it would seem sometimes as though Pussy required to have all her nine lives at her disposal, and yet runs some risk of being killed even then. Upon the vessel in which this gentleman served there was a black Cat that had lost its tail in rather a singular manner.

"A squall came on one night, and I gave the order to let go the main-top-gallant halyard. The Cat was in the coil of rope, and in whizzing through the leading block the rope cut off its tail. She remembered the place which she had found so dangerous, and could never afterwards be induced to venture abaft the foremast.

"In Sydney we had hauled out from Campbell's Wharf to the stream, previous to sailing next day for England, and found, when the men had gone to bed, that the tailless black Cat was missing. It could not be below, as the hatches were battened down. About 3 A.M. next morning, the two men who kept anchor watch heard a piteous cry at the bows, and looking over saw a black object clinging to the chain cable, trying to get in at the hawse-pipe. One of them lowered himself down by a bowline, and handed up poor Pussy in an awful plight. She had swum off to the ship,—about three hundred yards. It took three or four days of nursing before she recovered, but she got ronnd at last, and remained in the ship for more than five years afterwards.

"Sailors have the greatest objection to a Cat being thrown overboard. The captain one day found a Cat sitting on his chronometer in his cabin, and in a passion flung the Cat into the sea, although this cruel act was protested against by the man at the wheel and other men at work on the poop, who said that we should have an unlucky passage of it. This proved to be the case. We lost three men and a boy, besides our jibboom and fore-top-gallant mast, and we also ran short of water. All this the sailors — (they were North country men)—ascribed to the Cat's murder.

"As a rule, sailors treat Cats well, as they are sources of great amusement on board. One of the boys once took a Cat to the fore royal mast-head, and left it there. In about half-an-hour it was on deck again. It came down backwards, crying pitifully all the time. It never allowed the boy to touch it afterwards."

The same gentleman tells me that in Coburg, Canada West, he knew a widow lady who had a Cat two feet in height, and beautifully marked. It was supposed to be a cross-breed between a wild and a domestic Cat, His youngest brother has often ridden on it when eight years old. It was very docile. It had been fed highly when young, and never showed the least desire to hunt mice or birds, or to leave the house.

With regard to the origin of the name "Cat-o'-

nine tails," referred to in a former chapter, a writer in *Notes and Queries* says :—

" As there appears to be some uncertainty about the number of cords or tails attached to this whip, it may be a question whether, like its namesake, the animal, it did not originally commence by having only *one* tail, and in course of time or fashion increase to *nine*, the number of lives proverbially allotted to our domestic friend Pussy.

" According to the Talmudists (*Maccoth* iii. 10), the Jews, in carrying out their sentences of scourges, employed for that purpose a whip which had three lashes (Jahn's Arch. Biblica, page 247), and it is stated in the *Merlinus Liberatus*, or *John Partridge's Almanack for* 1692, that in " May, 1685, Dr. Oates was whipt," and " had 2,256 lashes with a whip of six thongs knotted, which amounts to 13,536 stripes." Sir John Vanbrugh, moreover, in the prologue to his play of the *False Friend* (written A.D. 1702), alludes to this scourge in these words:—

> " You dread reformers of an injurious age,
> You awful cat-o'-nine tails of the stage."

" In *James's Military Dictionary*, the cat, etc., is described as " a whip with nine knotted cords, with which the public soldiers and sailors are

punished. Sometimes it has only *five* cords."
The following passage occurs in Mr. Sala's *Waterloo
to the Peninsula :*—"A Dutch king, they say, introduced the cat-o'-nine tails in the British army : ere
the Nassauer's coming the scourge had *three*
thongs."

There is a little story of feline affection for
which I should have found a place in an earlier
chapter. A lady had a Cat which she called " the
Methodist Parson." It used for years regularly to
go away every Sunday morning, and return to its
home on the next (the Monday) morning. It was
never known to miss for a series of years, going
away on the Sunday morning, except upon one
occasion, when it stopped at home on the Sunday,
and went away on the Monday morning. After
this it never returned. In the same lady's house
upon a certain occasion, for some reason or other,
the water was turned off. It was in the evening,
and she had the tap of the water-butt turned on,
with a tub under it, thinking they would get water
when they wanted it. The family went to bed,
forgetting that the water-tap was left turned on.
In the course of the night the Cat came to the
lady's bedroom door, making a great noise, mewing.
Her husband got up several times, and drove it

away, but it returned again, and would go to the corner of the stairs, and then turn round, as if to see ,whether he was following it. At last he followed it down-stairs, and found the whole of the lower premises inundated, the water having been turned on from the main.

Here, too, is a facetious story, which should not be omitted :—

One night, some hours after a certain family had retired to rest, there arose a most extraordinary and unaccountable noise in the lower part of the house. Had thieves broken in? If so they must have been very noisy thieves, and quite careless as to the noise they made. You can imagine Paterfamilias sitting up in bed, and listening with suspended breath ; Materfamilias suggesting that he had better get up, and see what was the matter ; Paterfamilias of the contrary opinion, and inclined to wait a-while, and see what happened next. Then a group of white figures, with whiter faces, at the head of the stairs, and the mysterious noise below growing louder and louder.

But the explanation of all this was simple enough, when some venturesome spirit summoned up courage to creep down-stairs and enquire into the cause. The servant, when she had gone to bed, had left a strong brown jug on the dresser, with a drain of milk in the bottom of it After everyone had retired, Puss commenced prowling about, and, attracted by the milk in the bottom of the jug, put her head into it. Now, though the top of the jug was wide enough for the Cat to put her head through, it was not so wide but what it required a slight pressure for her to get her head into it. When the milk was lapped, however, she could not get her head out again, for it required some one to hold the jug, to enable her to do so. In the meantime, all being in bed and asleep, the Cat in her terror jumped about, knocking its head, with the jug on it, against the tables and chairs, and upon the kitchen floor. Hence the alarming and unaccountable disturbance.

I clip this from an American paper :—

" During the progress of the war I was sitting one day in the office of Able and Co.'s wharf-boat at Cairo, Illinois. At that time a tax was collected on all goods shipped south by private parties, and it was necessary that duplicate invoices of ship-ments should be furnished to the collector before the permits could be issued. The ignorance of this fact by many shippers frequently caused them much annoyance, and invoices were ofttimes made

out with great haste, in order to ensure shipment by boats on the eve of departure. A sutler, with a lot of stores, had made out a hasty list of his stock, and gave it to one of the youngest clerks on the boat to copy out in due form. The boy worked away down the list, but suddenly he stopped, and electrified the whole office by exclaiming, in a voice of undisguised amazement,—
'What the dickens is that fellow going to do with four boxes of Tom Cats?' An incredulous laugh from the other clerks was the reply, but the boy pointed triumphantly to the list, exclaiming, 'That's what it is—T-o-m C-a-t-s—Tom Cats, if I know how to read!' The entrance of the sutler at that moment explained the mystery.

"'Why, confound it!' said he, 'that means four boxes Tomato Catsup! Don't you understand abbreviations?'"

Here is a bit of my own experience :—

I once had in my possession a very life-like engraving of a remarkably ugly bulldog, which hung in a frame over a piano in the drawing-room. With some surprise I noticed, upon several occasions, that a favourite cat would climb upon the top of the piano, and sitting close underneath the picture, fix its eyes upon the dog's face, and

putting back its ears, remain **thus**, with a wild and
terrified expression, for as long as an hour at **a**
time. This was remarked by other persons in the
house, and we could not in any way satisfactorily
account for Puss's behaviour. Two dogs formed
part of the household, and with these she was on
friendly terms, and they being of a very meek and
harmless nature, she treated them with contempt,
as a general rule, boxing their ears now and then,
when their presence annoyed her. We came to the
conclusion, however, that she must have taken the
picture for another dog of a different and higher
order, more terrible in its motionless silence than if
it had growled or barked ever so fiercely. Its eyes
were drawn in that particular angle which made
them seem to be fixed upon you in whatever part
of the room you might be in. Many of us recollect
in our childhood some gaunt-featured oil-painting,
with hungry eyes, which thus pursued us. I
remember one in a scrap-book, which it wanted
some courage to face all by onesself, when twilight
was gathering. With much of the same shrinking
dread Puss seemed, whilst hating, to be unable to
break the spell this picture had over her, to the
contemplation of which she returned again and
again, though frequently sent away. During the

time that we noticed this conduct on the Cat's part, she was with Kitten, and when the four Kittens were born they were dead, and one of them, strange to say, had a bulldog-shaped head, marked almost exactly like the picture.

I need not tell a kind master or mistress to use every precaution when drowning a Cat's kittens, to keep their mother in ignorance of the fact. It can easily be imagined that the poor creature will be in great distress if the slaughter be committed before her eyes; and I know of a case where the Cat having found her young ones which had been drowned and thrown carelessly in the corner of a yard, brought the bodies back to her nest, and mewing and licking them, seemed to use every endeavour to restore them to life. A friend of mine, too, once passing along the bank of a river one moonlight night found a Cat mewing piteously among the long grass at the water's edge. He came to a stand-still a dozen yards from the spot, and looked on curiously. At sight of him, the Cat turned round, and came running to his feet, looking-up appealingly into his face, and running back to the water side and then back again to him, seemingly to be entreating his assistance. Presently the moonlight showed him three or four kittens being borne away by the

TO THE RESCUE.

stream, and crying in small weak voices for their mother's help. He did everything in his power to reach them, but they were too far away from the bank, and very soon they came to a place where the current was stronger, and swept them out of sight. The mother's cries were then most heart-rending, and he was unable to induce her to come away. Indeed, having taken her in his arms, and carried her some distance, she struggled and fought violently to regain her liberty, and ran back again to the water's edge. This took place at some distance from any habitation, but he concluded that somebody must have thrown the kittens into the water, and that the Cat had followed them, and seen the deed done.

There are some children who will not cry, however much they are beaten; it is as difficult to make a Cat cry out when you chastise it. It will shrink; sometimes growl; but rarely cry: yet when beaten by another Cat, it will howl loudly. A dog on the contrary, very often cries at the bare sight of the whip, and screams at the lightest blow.

Some people say all Cats are thieves. I will not deny that a good many are: indeed, so are dogs. Neither will steal much if they are well fed, as they only take food when they are hungry. Here, however, is a plan by which, I think, you can generally ascertain whether or not a Cat is of a thievish disposition. Give the Cat a piece of meat an inch square, and if he is a dishonest rascal, he will not lay it down on the floor to pick it up again as is the usual way with his species, but keep tight hold of it with his teeth, and jerk it down his throat, sometimes using his paws to prevent its falling.

There is one ridiculous accusation brought against poor Pussy, which I have not yet referred to, namely, that she is in the habit, when the opportunity offers, of suffocating young babies by sucking their breath. Now, since the world began, I beg emphatically to state, no baby was ever so suffocated, and I say this in the face of numerous newspaper paragraphs, and a thousand old women's stories :—

For instance, *the " Annual Register,"* January 25, 1791, says :—

A child of eighteen months old, was found dead near Plymouth ; and it appeared, on the coroner's inquest, " that the child died in consequence of a Cat sucking its breath, thereby occasioning a strangulation."

My friend Mr. Burrows, surgeon, of Westbourne

Park Place, who is a great lover of animals, gives me this note:—

" It is quite impossible for a Cat to suck a child's breath, as the anatomical formation of the Cat's mouth would prevent it. No doubt in some remote country places, among the ignorant, a popular superstition to that effect may exist, but when a child has been found dead from suffocation, in many cases the Cat may have lain on the infant's mouth, in the cot or cradle near the fire, for the sake of warmth—not with the slightest criminal intent of course, but purely for the sake of obtaining the latent caloric from the warm body and clothing of the infant, who would probably not possess sufficient muscular power to disencumber itself, or even to make any resistance."

But it is not only in remote country places that the superstition prevails, but here in London, among most of the upper middle classes. And after all, are not more ridiculous notions to be met with every day? Only a few months ago, a lady was seriously informed by a poor woman in a village near Bath, that a mother should never cut her child's nails before it is a year old. She should always bite them, otherwise the children would grow up thieves.

U

In Ireland, the following cure for warts is practised by even the most intelligent classes :— "Take a small stone, less than a boy's marble for each wart, and tie them in a clean linen bag, and throw it out on the highway. Then find out a stone in some field or ditch with a hollow in which rain or dew may have lodged (such stones are easily found in rural districts), and wash the warts seven times therein, and after this operation, whoever picks up the bag of stones will have a transfer of the warts."

Here again is a little bit of Devonshire Folk-lore which has its believers :—"When you see the new moon in the new year, take your stocking off from one foot, and run to the next stile; when you get there, between the great toe and the next, you will find a hair which will be the colour of your lover's." This must be rare sport while there is snow on the ground.

There is also a vulgar superstition to the effect that a Cat left in the room with a dead body will fly at and disfigure the face of the corpse. Some of my readers may remember the old man's death in "Bleak House," and how the Cat was carefully shut out of the room where the body lay. From what I recollect, Cats are not great favourites of

Mr. Dickens', though "Dickens' Dogs," a small collection from his canine heroes, published some years ago, showed him to be a great lover and close observer of that animal.

Pope says:—

> "But thousands die without or this or that—
>   Die and endow a college or a Cat."

The latter case, however, is rather rare I should think. When Pussy's good master and mistress die, the wide world is often enough left for it to roam in at its will, seeking its living as it can — a wide world full of cruel kicks and cuffs. Justin's Cat was lucky to die of old age in a good home, and have such a fine epitaph written over his remains:—

> Worn out with age and dire disease, a Cat,
> Friendly to all save wicked mouse and rat,
> I'm sent at last to ford the Stygian lake,
> And to the infernal coast a voyage make.
> Me Proserpine received, and smiling said,
> "Be bless'd within these mansions of the dead;
> Enjoy among thy velvet-footed loves,
> Elysium's sunny banks and shady groves."
> "But if I've well deserved (O gracious Queen)—
> If patient under suffering I have been,
> Grant me at least one night to visit home again,

Once more to see my home and mistress dear,
And purr these grateful accents in her ear.
' Thy faithful Cat, thy poor departed slave,
Still loves her mistress e'en beyond the grave.' "

Stray Cats, I am afraid, have a bad time of it before they find a new home. Cats were recently said to be in great demand at Lucerne, in Switzerland, and to be selling at a high price, in consequence of a malady which had greatly thinned their numbers. According to the account in the newspaper, the head of the animal swelled rapidly; the Cat refused all nourishment, and very soon dropped down dead.

It is true, that in some quarters of the globe, the feline race is still held of some value. *Vide* Lady Duff Gordon's Article in *Macmillan's Magazine*, which gives us a glimpse of a strange superstition in Thebes. She says :—

" Do you remember the German story of the lad who travelled ' um das gruseln zu lernen ' (to learn how to tremble) ? Well, I who never ' gruselte ' (quaked) before, had a touch of it a few mornings ago. I was sitting here quietly drinking tea, and four or five men were present, when a Cat came to the door. I called ' bis ! bis !' and offered milk ; but puss, after looking at us, ran away.

"'Well, dost thou, Lady,' said a quiet sensible man, a merchant here, 'to be kind to the Cat, for I daresay he gets little enough at home ; *his* father, poor man, cannot cook for his children every day ;' and then in an explanatory tone to the company : 'That's Alec Nasseeree's boy, Yussuf ; it must be Yussuf, because his fellow-twin, Ismaeen, is with his uncle at Negadeh.'

"'Mir gruselte' (I shuddered), I confess ; not but what I have heard things almost as absurd from gentlemen and ladies in Europe, but an 'extravagance' in a kuftan has quite a different effect from one in a tail-coat.

"'What! My butcher-boy who brings the meat— a Cat ?' I gasped.

"'To be sure, and he knows well where to look for a bit of good cookery, you see. All twins go out as Cats at night, if they go to sleep hungry ; and their own bodies lie at home like dead, meanwhile, but no one must touch them or they would die. When they grow up to ten or twelve they leave it off. Why, your own boy, Achmet, does it. Ho, Achmet !'

"Achmet appears.

"'Boy, don't you go out as a Cat at night ?'

"'No,' said Achmet tranquilly, 'I am not a twin. My sister's sons do.'

"I enquired if people were not afraid of such Cats.

" 'No, there is no fear ; they only eat a little of the cookery ; but if you beat them, they tell their parents next day. 'So and so beat me in his house last night,' and show their bruises. No, they are not afreets ; they are beni-Adam. Only twins do it, and if you give them a sort of onion broth and some milk, the first thing when they are born, they do not do it at all.'

"Omar professed never to have heard it, but I am sure he had, only he dreads being laughed at. One of the American missionaries told me something like it, as belonging to the Copts; but it is entirely Egyptian, and common to both religions. I asked several Copts, who assured me it was true, and told it just the same. Is it a remnant of the doctrine of transmigration ? However, the notion fully accounts for the horror the people feel at the idea of killing a Cat."

Ah, heaven help those whom we love and cherish when we are dead and gone! The soft, delicate hands that never were made to work—the gentle hearts untried — the pretty, thoughtless heads, pillowed so softly, slumbering so placidly, all unconscious that there is a rough, unsympathising crowd surging round the castle gates, whose hoarse murmur has never yet reached our darlings' ears. And our dumb pets, where shall they find a home, and kind hands to wait upon them? It is a thousand times better when we die that they should die too ; and you, whose roof has sheltered a Cat, should you change your home, and be unable to take the creature with you, would act a more humane part by having it killed at once than leave it to the questionable mercy of the new comer. The too often carelessly uttered words of " Oh, the Cat will get on well enough," have sealed the poor dependant's fate, and it has been left to shift for itself, with what fate its late owners have but rarely troubled themselves to enquire. What fate would many of us meet with were not a helping hand stretched forth in time of need? To how many of our poor brothers and sisters is the help never tendered!

There is a hospital for dogs, which is, I am told, in a flourishing condition ; and a lady of the name of Deen established a sort of asylum for lost Cats at Rottingdean, in consequence of the large number which she saw lying dead upon the beach, and, indeed, offered premiums to anyone who would bring animals of the feline species to her city of refuge. But such kind friends are scarce, and Pussy, going upon her travels, will find many dangers upon the road, and but few doors opened to receive her. Therefore, in conclusion, I would advise all Cats to stay at home when they have a good home to stay at. One word, too, I would fain say to those who do not like Cats, because they do not know them. Having long observed these animals carefully, and, I sincerely believe, without prejudice, I am sure that when kindly treated they will be found gentle and attached, and little, if at all, inferior in intelligence to their much-vaunted rival, the dog. One last word to those who have followed me thus far. I hope I have not been very prosy, and I hope, in the somewhat large collection of Cat anecdotes here brought together, " the only one worth the trouble of relating " has not been omitted. If this has been the case, allow me to assure you it has not been because I have spared any trouble in gathering together my materials.

THE END.

ORIGINAL JUVENILE LIBRARY.

A CATALOGUE

OF

NEW AND POPULAR WORKS,

PRINCIPALLY FOR THE YOUNG.

Goldsmith Introduced to Newbery by Dr. Johnson.

PUBLISHED BY

GRIFFITH AND FARRAN,

(SUCCESSORS TO NEWBERY AND HARRIS),

CORNER OF ST. PAUL'S CHURCHYARD,
LONDON.

WERTHEIMER, LEA AND CO., CIRCUS PLACE, FINSBURY CIRCUS.

A SPLENDID GIFT BOOK.

*Dedicated by Permission to H.R.H. The Princess Royal. In Royal 4to.,
Elegantly bound in cloth, gilt edges. Price Two Guineas.*

The Year: its Leaves and Blossoms;

Illustrated by HENRY STILKE, in Thirteen Beautiful Chromo-Lithographic Plates, with Verses from the Poets.

"A charming Gift Book, and sure to be heartily welcomed."—*Art Union.*

STANESBY'S ILLUMINATED GIFT BOOKS.

Every page richly printed in Gold and Colours.

The Floral Gift.

Small 4to, price 14s. cloth elegant; 21s. morocco extra.

"Every page has a border printed in Gold and Colours, in which our chief floral favourites are admirably depicted. The binding is gorgeous, yet in good taste."—*Gentleman's Magazine.*

Aphorisms of the Wise and Good.

With a Photographic Portrait of Milton. Price 9s. cloth, elegant; 14s. Turkey morocco antique.

"A perfect gem in binding, illustration, and literary excellence."—*Daily News.*

Shakespeare's Household Words;

With a Photographic Portrait taken from the Monument at Stratford-on-Avon. Price 9s. cloth elegant; 14s. morocco antique.

"An exquisite little gem, fit to be the Christmas offering to Titania or Queen Mab."—*The Critic.*

The Wisdom of Solomon;

From the Book of Proverbs. Small 4to, price 14s. cloth elegant: 18s. calf; 21s. morocco antique.

"The borders are of surprising richness and variety, and the colours beautifully blended."—*Morning Post.*

The Bridal Souvenir;

New Edition, with a Portrait of the Princess Royal. Elegantly bound in white and gold, price 21s.

"A splendid specimen of decorative art, and well suited for a bridal gift."—*Literary Gazette.*

The Birth-Day Souvenir;

A Book of Thoughts on Life and Immortality. Small 4to. price 12s. 6d. illuminated cloth; 18s. morocco antique.

"The illuminations are admirably designed.—*Gentleman's Magazine.*

Light for the Path of Life;

From the Holy Scriptures. Small 4to, price 12s. cloth elegant, 15s. calf, gilt edges; 18s. morocco antique.

NEW AND POPULAR WORKS.

NEW WORK BY JOHN TIMBS.

Ancestral Stories and Traditions of Great Families.

Illustrative of English History. By John Timbs, F.S.A. With Frontispiece. Post 8vo., price 7s. 6d., cloth elegant.

NEW WORK BY BARBARA HUTTON.

Heroes of the Crusades.

By Barbara Hutton, author of "Castles and their Heroes." Illustrated by Priolo. Post 8vo., 5s. Cloth elegant, 5s. 6d., gilt edges.

NEW WORK BY CAPTAIN DRAYSON.

Adventures of Hans Sterk.

The South African Hunter and Pioneer. By Captain Drayson, author of "Tales of the Outspan," etc. Illustrated by Zwecker. Post 8vo., price 5s. Cloth elegant, 5s. 6d., gilt edges.

NEW ILLUSTRATED EDITION.

Trimmer's History of the Robins.

Written for the Instruction of Children on their treatment of Animals. With 24 beautiful Engravings from Drawings by Harrison Weir. Price 6s. Cloth extra, 7s. 6d. Cloth elegant, gilt edges.

NEW WORK BY KAY SPEN.

Our White Violet.

By Kay Spen, author of "Gerty and May," with Illustrations by T. S. Wale. Super Royal 16mo., price 2s. 6d. cloth elegant, 3s. 6d. coloured, gilt edges.

ILLUSTRATED BY FRÖLICH.

The Little Gipsy.

By ELIE SAUVAGE. Translated by ANNA BLACKWELL. Profusely illustrated by LORENZ FRÖLICH. Small 4to., price 5s. cloth elegant, 6s. gilt edges.

Neptune.

The Autobiography of a Newfoundland Dog. By the author of "Tuppy," &c. Illustrated by A. T. ELWES. Super Royal 16mo., price 2s. 6d. cloth elegant, 3s. 6d. coloured, gilt edges.

NEW WORK BY MRS. DAVENPORT.

Constance and Nellie;

Or, the Lost Will. By EMMA DAVENPORT, author of "Our Birthdays," &c. Frontispiece by T. S. WALE. Fcap. 8vo., price 2s. 6d. cloth elegant, 3s. gilt edges.

NEW WORK BY CAPTAIN MARRYAT'S DAUGHTER.

Stolen Cherries;

Or, Tell the Truth at Once. By EMILIA MARRYAT NORRIS. Illustrated by F. A. FRASER. Super Royal 16mo., price 2s. 6d. cloth, 3s. 6d. coloured, gilt edges.

NEW WORK BY HOOD'S DAUGHTER.

Tales of the Toys.

Told by Themselves. By FRANCES FREELING BRODERIP. With Illustrations by her brother, TOM HOOD. Super Royal 16mo., price 3s. 6d. cloth elegant, 4s. 6d. coloured, gilt edges.

Alice and Beatrice.

By GRANDMAMMA. With Illustrations by JOHN ABSOLON. Super Royal 16mo., price 2s. 6d. cloth elegant, 3s. 6d. coloured, gilt edges.

Corner Cottage and its Inmates;

Or, Trust in God. By FRANCES OSBORNE. With Illustrations by the Author. Fcap. 8vo., price 2s. 6d. cloth elegant, 3s. gilt edges.

Sunbeam, a Fairy Tale.

By MRS. PIETZKER. With Illustrations by ALEXANDER CHARLEMAGNE. Small Post 8vo., price 3s. 6d. cloth elegant.

The Confessions of a Lost Dog,

Reported by her Mistress, FRANCES POWER COBBE. With a Photograph of the Dog from Life, by FRANK HAES. Super-royal 16mo, price 2s. cloth, gilt edges.

His Name was Hero.

Frontispiece from a Painting by SIR W. CALCOTT, R.A. Price 1s. sewed.

BY THE SAME AUTHOR.

The Grateful Sparrow.

A True Story, with Frontispiece. Fifth Edition. Price 6d. sewed.

How I Became a Governess.

Third Edition. With Frontispiece. Price 2s. cloth, 2s. 6d. gilt edges.

Dicky Birds.

A True Story. Third Edition. With Frontispiece. Price 6d.

My Pretty Puss.

With Frontispiece. Price 6d.

The Adventures of a Butterfly.

From the French of P. J. STAHL. Seven Engravings. Price 8d.

The Hare that Found his Way Home.

From the French of P. J. STAHL. With Frontispiece. Price 6d.

CHARLES BENNETT'S LAST WORK.

Lightsome and the Little Golden Lady.

Written and Illustrated by C. H. BENNETT. Twenty-four Engravings. Fcap. 4to., price 3s. 6d. cloth elegant; 4s. 6d. coloured, gilt edges.

" The work of a man who is sure to put some touch of a peculiar genius into whatever he does."— *Pall Mall Gazette.*

" There is rare fun for the little ones, and there is genius in the fun."— *Nonconformist.*

WORKS BY JOHN TIMBS.

Lady Bountiful's Legacy

To her Family and Friends: a Book of Practical Instructions and Duties, Counsels and Experiences, Hints and Recipes in Housekeeping and Domestic Management. Post 8vo, price 6s. cloth elegant; 7s. bevelled boards, gilt edges.

"When it is remembered that the sum total of our worldly happiness rests with the comforts and amenities of home life, the true value of the teaching in this book cannot fail of being fully appreciated."—*Morning Post.*

"There is something to be found in this volume about everything which concerns the household."—*Churchman.*

Nooks and Corners of English Life.

Past and Present. By JOHN TIMBS. With Illustrations. Post 8vo, price 6s. cloth; 6s. 6d. gilt edges.

"There is not a chapter in the whole work in which instructive matter is not found."—*London Review.*

"A book which ought to find a place in one of the nooks and 'corners' of every library."—*The Reliquary.*

Strange Stories of the Animal World;

A Book of Adventures and Anecdotes, and curious Contributions to Natural History. By JOHN TIMBS. Illustrations by ZWECKER, Post 8vo., price 6s., cloth, 6s. 6d., gilt edges.

"Among all the books of the season that will be studied with profit and pleasure, there is not one more meritorious in aim, or more successful in execution."—*Athenæum.*

Casimir, the Little Exile.

By CAROLINE PEACHEY. With Illustrations by C. STANTON. Post 8vo., price 4s. 6d. cloth elegant; 5s. gilt edges.

"The tone of 'Casimir' is healthy, and the story will be found no less beneficial than interesting."—*Athenæum.*

Lucy's Campaign;

A Story of Adventure. By MARY and CATHERINE LEE. With Illustrations by GEORGE HAY. Fcap. 8vo, price 3s. cloth elegant; 3s. 6d. gilt edges.

"The adventures 'Lucy' goes through are detailed in a remarkably agreeable manner."—*The Queen.*

Gerty and May.

By the Author of "Granny's Story Box," and "Our White Violet." Illustrated by M. L. VINING. Price 2s. 6d. cloth; 3s. 6d. coloured, gilt edges.

"A charming book for children. Though the story is full of fun, the moral is never lost sight of."—*Literary Churchman*.

Nursery Times;

Or, Stories about the Little Ones. By an Old Nurse. Illustrated by J. LAWSON. Price 3s. 6d. cloth; 4s. 6d. coloured, gilt edges.

Animals and Birds;

Sketches from Nature by Harrison Weir, for the use of the Young Artist. Royal 4to., publishing in parts, price 1s. each.

*** Parts I. and II. now ready.

BY THE HON. MISS BETHELL.

Helen in Switzerland.

By the Hon. AUGUSTA BETHELL. With Illustrations by E. WHYMPER. Super-royal 16mo, price 3s. 6d. cloth extra; 4s. 6d. coloured, gilt edges.

"A pleasant variety of local legend and history, mingled with the incidents of travel." —*The Spectator*.

Echoes of an Old Bell;

And other Tales of Fairy Lore, by the Honble. AUGUSTA BETHELL. Illustrations by F. W. KEYL. Super royal 16mo., price 3s. 6d. cloth, 4s. 6d. coloured, gilt edges.

"A delightful book of well-conceived and elegantly-written fairy tales."—*Literary Churchman*.

The Surprising Adventures of the Clumsy Boy

CRUSOE. By CHARLES H. Ross. With Twenty-three Coloured Illustrations. Imperial 8vo, price 2s.

Infant Amusements;

Or, How to Make a Nursery Happy. With Hints to Parents and Nurses on the Moral and Physical Training of Children. By W. H. G. KINGSTON. Post 8vo, price 3s. 6d. cloth.

"We urge parents most strongly to obtain this book forthwith; we know of no book that can compare with it in practical value. Each chapter is worth the price of the book."—*Our Fireside*.

Taking Tales for Cottage Homes;

in Plain Language and Large Type. In Twelve Parts, each containing Sixty-four pages, and several Engravings. 4d. each. Complete in Four Volumes, cloth, 1s. 6d., or 2 vols. extra cloth, 3s. 6d each.

" The terse Saxon terms employed are level to the capacity of the humblest."—*Ragged School Magazine.*
" Written in a clear and sensible style."—*Guardian.*

Featherland;

Or, How the Birds lived at Greenlawn. By G. W. FENN. With Illustrations by F. W. KEYL. Super-royal 16mo., price 2s. 6d., cloth, 3s. 6d., coloured, gilt edges.

" A delightful book for children. There is no story, but the happiest perception of childish enjoyment is contained in fanciful sketches of bird-life."—*Examiner.*

The Australian Babes in the Wood;

A True Story told in Rhyme for the Young. With Illustrations by HUGH CAMERON, A.R.S.A.; J. McWHIRTIE; GEO. HAY; J. LAWSON, &c. Imperial 16mo. 1s. 6d. Boards. 2s. Cloth, gilt edges.

Trottie's Story Book;

True Tales in Short Words and Large Type. Eight Illustrations by WEIR. Price 2s. 6d., cloth, 3s. 6d., coloured, gilt edges.

Tiny Stories for Tiny Readers in Tiny Words.

With Twelve Illustrations by HARRISON WEIR. Third edition. Price 2s. 6d. cloth, 3s. 6d. coloured, gilt edges.

Work in the Colonies;

Some Account of the Missionary operations of the Church of England in connexion with the Society for the Propagation of the Gospel in Foreign Parts. With Map and Sixteen Illustrations. Royal 16mo. price 5s., cloth.

Early Days of English Princes;

By Mrs. RUSSELL GRAY. Illustrations by JOHN FRANKLIN. New and Enlarged Edition. Super-royal 16mo., price 3s. 6d., cloth, 4s. 6d., coloured, gilt edges.

Pictures of Girl Life.

By CATHARINE AUGUSTA HOWELL. Frontispiece by F. ELTZE. Fcap. 8vo., price 3s. cloth, 3s. 6d. gilt edges.

" A really healthy and stimulating book for girls."—*Nonconformist.*

Pages of Child Life;

By CATHARINE AUGUSTA HOWELL. With Three Illustrations. Fcap. 8vo., price 3s. 6d. cloth.

The Four Seasons.

A Short Account of the Structure of Plants, being Four Lectures written for the Working Men's Institute, Paris. With Illustrations. Imperial 16mo. Price, 3s 6d. cloth.

"Distinguished by extreme clearness, and teeming with information of a useful and popular character."--*Guardian.*

Fun and Earnest;

Or, Rhymes with Reason, by D'ARCY W. THOMPSON. Illustrated by CHARLES H. BENNETT. Imperial 16mo., price 3s. cloth, 4s. 6d. coloured. Cloth, Elegant gilt edges.

"Only a clever man with the touch of a poet's feeling in him, can write good children's nonsense; such a man the author proves himself to be."--*Examiner.*

Nursery Nonsense;

Or Rhymes without Reason, by D'ARCY W. THOMPSON, with sixty Illustrations, by C. H. BENNETT. Second edition. Imperial 16mo., price 2s. 6d. cloth; or 4s. 6d. coloured, cloth elegant, gilt edges.

"The funniest book we have seen for an age, and quite as harmless as hearty."—*Daily Review.*

"Whatever Mr. Bennett does, has some touch in it of a true genius."—*Examiner.*

Spectropia;

Or, Surprising Spectral Illusions, showing Ghosts everywhere and of any Colour. By J. H. BROWN. Fifth edition. Quarto. Coloured Plates. Price 2s. 6d. fancy boards.

"One of the best scientific toy books we have seen."—*Athenæum.*

"A clever book. The illusions are founded on true scientific principles."—*Chemical News.*

WORKS BY LADY LUSHINGTON.

Almeria's Castle;

Or, My Early Life in India and England. By LADY LUSHINGTON, with Twelve Illustrations. Price 4s. 6d., cloth, 5s., gilt edges.

"The Authoress has a very graphic pen, and brings before our eyes, with singular vividness, the localities and modes of life she aims to describe."—*London Review.*

Hacco the Dwarf;

Or, The Tower on the Mountain; and other Tales, by LADY LUSHINGTON. Illustrated by G. J. PINWELL. Super royal 16mo., price 3s. 6d. cloth, 4s. 6d. coloured, gilt edges.

"Enthusiasm is not our usual fashion, but the excellence of these stories is so greatly above the average of most clever tales for the play-room, that we are tempted to reward the author with admiration."--*Athenæum.*

The Happy Home;

Or the Children at the Red House, by LADY LUSHINGTON. Illustrated by G. J. PINWELL. Price 3s. 6d. cloth, 4s. 6d. coloured, gilt edges.

"A happy mixture of fact and fiction. Altogether it is one of the best books of the kind we have met with."—*Guardian.*

BY MRS. HENRY WOOD.

William Allair;

Or, Running away to Sea, by Mrs. H. Wood, author of "The Channings," etc. Frontispiece by F. Gilbert. Second edition. Fcap. 8vo., price 2s. 6d., cloth, 3s. gilt edges.

"There is a fascination about Mrs. Wood's writings, from which neither old nor young can escape."—*Bell's Messenger.*

WORKS BY MRS. DAVENPORT.

The Holidays Abroad;

Or, Right at Last. By Emma Davenport. With Frontispiece by G. Hay. Fcap. 8vo., price 2s. 6d. cloth extra; 3s. gilt edges.

"Its tone is healthy and natural."—*Churchman.*

The Happy Holidays;

Or, Brothers and Sisters at Home, by Emma Davenport. Frontispiece by F. Gilbert. Fcap. 8vo., price 2s. 6d. cloth, 3s. gilt edges.

Our Birth Days;

And how to improve them, by Mrs. E. Davenport, Frontispiece by D. H. Friston. Fcap. 8vo., price 2s. 6d. cloth, 3s. gilt edges.

"Most admirably suited as a gift to young girls."—*British Mother's Magazine.*

Fickle Flora,

And her Sea Side Friends. By Emma Davenport. With Illustrations by J. Absolon. Price 3s. 6d. cloth; 4s. 6d. coloured, gilt edges

Live Toys;

Or, Anecdotes of our Four-legged and other Pets. By Emma Davenport. With Illustrations by Harrison Weir. Second Edition. Super Royal 16mo. price 2s. 6d. cloth; 3s. 6d. coloured, gilt edges.

"One of the best kind of books for youthful reading."—*Guardian.*

DEDICATED BY PERMISSION TO ROSSINI.

Little by Little.

A series of Graduated Lessons in the Art of Reading Music. Second Edition. Oblong 8vo., price 3s. 6d. cloth.

"One of the best productions of the kind which have yet appeared."—*Charles Steggall, Mus. D., Cantab.*

Memorable Battles in English History.

Where Fought, why Fought, and their Results. With Lives of the Commanders. By W. H. Davenport Adams. Frontispiece by Robert Dudley. Post 8vo. price 6s. extra cloth.

"Of the care and honesty of the author's labours, the book gives abundant proof."—*Athenæum.*

The Loves of Tom Tucker and Little Bo-Peep.

Written and Illustrated by Tom Hood. Quarto, price 2s. 6d. coloured plates.

"Full of fun and of good innocent humour. The Illustrations are excellent."—*The Critic.*

WORKS BY M. BETHAM EDWARDS.

The Primrose Pilgrimage.

A Woodland Story, by M. Betham Edwards, illustrations by T. R. Macquoid. Price 2s. 6d. cloth, 3s. 6d. coloured, gilt edges.

"One of the best books of children's verse that has appeared since the early days of Mary Howitt."—*Nonconformist.*
" The Poems are full of interest, and the Illustrations charming."—*Art Journal.*

Scenes and Stories of the Rhine.

By M. Betham Edwards. With Illustrations by F. W. Keyl. Price 3s. 6d. cloth; 4s. 6d. coloured, gilt edges.

"Full of amusing incidents, good stories, and sprightly pictures."—*The Dial.*

Holidays Among the Mountains;

Or, Scenes and Stories of Wales. By M. Betham Edwards. Illustrated by F. J. Skill. Price 3s. 6d. cloth; 4s. 6d. coloured, gilt edges.

Nursery Fun;

Or, the Little Folks' Picture Book. The Illustrations by C. H. Bennett. Quarto, price 2s. 6d. coloured plates.

" Will be greeted with shouts of laughter in any nursery."—*The Critic.*

Play-Room Stories;

Or, How to make Peace. By Georgiana M. Craik. With Illustrations by C. Green. Price 3s. 6d. cloth; 4s. 6d. coloured, gilt edges.

"This Book will come with 'peace' upon its wings into many a crowded playroom."
—*Art Journal.*

The Faithful Hound.

A Story in Verse, founded on fact. By Lady Thomas. With Illustrations by H. Weir. Imperial 16mo, price 2s. 6d. cloth; 3s. 6d. coloured, gilt edges.

Jack Frost and Betty Snow;

With other Tales for Wintry Nights and Rainy Days. Illustrated by H. Weir. Second Edition. 2s. 6d. cloth; 3s. 6d. coloured, gilt edges.

" The dedication of these pretty tales, prove by whom they are written; they are indelibly stamped with that natural and graceful method of amusing while instructing, which only persons of genius possess."—*Art Journal.*

BOOKS FOR BOYS.

With Illustrations, Fcap. 8vo. price 5s. each cloth.

Luke Ashleigh;

Or, School Life in Holland. By ALFRED ELWES.

"The author's best book, by a writer whose popularity with boys is great."—*Athenæum.*

Guy Rivers;

Or, a Boy's Struggles in the Great World. By A. ELWES.

Ralph Seabrooke;

Or, The Adventures of a Young Artist in Piedmont and Tuscany. By A. ELWES.

Frank and Andrea;

Or Forest Life in the Island of Sardinia. By A. ELWES.

Paul Blake;

Or, the Story of a Boy's Perils in the Islands of Corsica and Monte Christo. By A. ELWES.

Ocean and her Rulers;

A Narrative of the Nations who have held dominion over the Sea; and comprising a brief History of Navigation. By ALFRED ELWES.

Lost in Ceylon;

The Story of a Boy and Girl's Adventures in the Woods and Wilds of the Lion King of Kandy. By WILLIAM DALTON.

The White Elephant;

Or the Hunters of Ava. By WILLIAM DALTON.

The War Tiger;

Or, The Adventures and Wonderful Fortunes of the Young Sea-Chief and his Lad Chow. By W. DALTON.

"A tale of lively adventure vigorously told, and embodying much curious information." *Illustrated News.*

Neptune's Heroes : or The Sea Kings of England;

from Hawkins to Franklin. By W. H. DAVENPORT ADAMS.

"We trust Old England may ever have writers as ready and able to interpret to her children the noble lives of her greatest men."—*Athenæum.*

Historical Tales of Lancastrian Times.

By the Rev. H. P. DUNSTER, M.A.

"Conveys a good deal of information about the manners and customs of England and France in the 15th Century."—*Gentlemen's Magazine.*

The Fairy Tales of Science.

By J. C. BROUGH. With 16 Illustrations by C. H. BENNETT. New Edition, Revised throughout.

"Science, perhaps, was never made more attractive and easy of entrance into the youthful mind."—*The Builder.*

"Altogether the volume is one of the most original, as well as one of the most useful, books of the season."—*Gentleman's Magazine.*

WORKS BY THOMAS HOOD'S DAUGHTER.

Wild Roses;

Or, Simple Stories of Country Life. By FRANCIS FREELING BRODERIP. Illustrated by ANELAY. Post 8vo, 3s. 6d. cloth 4s. gilt edges.

"Written with the grace and truthfulness which the daughter of Tom Hood knows so well how to impart."—Art Journal.

Mamma's Morning Gossips;

Or, Little Bits for Little Birds. Containing Easy Lessons in Words of One Syllable, and Stories to read. With Fifty Illustrations by TOM HOOD. Foolscap Quarto, 3s., cloth, 4s. 6d. coloured, gilt edges.

Merry Songs for Little Voices;

The words by Mrs. BRODERIP; set to music by THOMAS MURBY, with 40 illustrations by TOM HOOD. Fcap. 4to., price 3s. cloth.

Crosspatch, the Cricket, and the Counterpane;

A Patchwork of Story and Song. Illustrated by TOM HOOD. Super royal 16mo. price 3s. 6d. cl., 4s. 6d. coloured, gilt edges.

"Hans Andersen has a formidable rival in this gentle lady."—Art Journal.

My Grandmother's Budget

of Stories and Verses. Illustrated by TOM HOOD. Price 3s. 6d. cloth; 4s. 6d. coloured, gilt edges.

"Some of the most charming little inventions that ever adorned the department of literature."—Illustrated Times.

Tiny Tadpole;

And other Tales. With Illustrations by TOM HOOD. Price 3s. 6d. cloth; 4s. 6d. coloured, gilt edges.

"A remarkable book, by the brother and sister of a family in which genius and fun are inherited."—Saturday Review.

Funny Fables for Little Folks.

Illustrated by TOM HOOD. Price 2s. 6d. cl.; 3s. 6d. col., gilt edges.

BY CAPTAIN MARRYAT'S DAUGHTER.

With Illustrations by various Artists. Super-royal 16mo, price 2s. 6d. each cloth elegant, 3s. 6d. coloured, gilt edges.

The Children's Pic Nic,

And what Came of it.

What became of Tommy;

By EMILIA MARRYAT NORRIS.

A Week by Themselves;

By EMILIA MARRYAT NORRIS.

"Our younger readers will be charmed with a story of some youthful Crusoes, written by the daughter of Captain Marryat."—Guardian.

Harry at School;

By EMILIA MARRYAT.

Long Evenings;

Or, Stories for My Little Friends. Second Edition.

LANDELL'S INSTRUCTIVE AND AMUSING WORKS.

The Boy's own Toy Maker.

A Practical Illustrated Guide to the useful employment of Leisure Hours. By E. LANDELLS. With Two Hundred Cuts. Seventh Edition. Royal 16mo, price 2s. 6d., cloth.

" A new and valuable form of endless amusement."—*Nonconformist.*

" We recommend it to all who have children to be instructed and amused."—*Economist.*

The Girl's Own Toy Maker,

And Book of Recreation. By E. and A. LANDELLS. Fourth Edition. With 200 Illustrations. Royal 16mo. price 2s. 6d. cloth.

" A perfect magazine of information."—*Illustrated News of the World.*

Home Pastime;

Or, The Child's Own Toy Maker. With practical instructions. By E. LANDELLS. New and Cheaper Edition, price 3s. 6d. complete, with the Cards, and Descriptive Letterpress.

. By this novel and ingenious "Pastime," Twelve beautiful Models can be made by Children from the Cards.

" As a delightful exercise of ingenuity, and a most sensible mode of passing a winter's evening, we commend the Child's own Toy Maker."—*Illustrated News.*

" Should be in every house blessed with the presence of children."—*The Field.*

The Illustrated Paper Model Maker;

Containing Twelve Pictorial Subjects, with Descriptive Letter-press and Diagrams for the construction of the Models. By E. LANDELLS. Price 2s. in a neat Envelope.

" A most excellent mode of educating both eye and hand in the knowledge of form."—*English Churchman.*

THE LATE THOMAS HOOD.

Fairy Land;

Or, Recreation for the Rising Generation, in Prose and Verse. By THOMAS and JANE HOOD. Illustrated by T. HOOD, Jun. Second Edition. Super-royal 16mo; price 3s. 6d. cloth; 4s. 6d. coloured gilt edges.

" These tales are charming. Before it goes into the Nursery, we recommend all grown up people should study ' Fairy Land.' "—*Blackwood.*

The Headlong Career and Woful Ending of Preco-

CIOUS PIGGY. Written for his Children, by the late THOMAS HOOD. With a Preface by his Daughter; and Illustrated by his Son. Fourth Edition. Post 4to, fancy boards, price 2s. 6d., coloured.

" The Illustrations are intensely humourous."—*The Critic.*

BY THE AUTHOR OF "TRIUMPHS OF STEAM," ETC.

Meadow Lea;

Or, the Gipsy Children; a Story founded on fact. With Illustrations by JOHN GILBERT. Fcap. 8vo. price 4s. 6d. cloth; 5s. gilt edges.

The Triumphs of Steam;

Or, Stories from the Lives of Watt, Arkwright, and Stephenson. With Illustrations by J. GILBERT. Dedicated by permission to Robert Stephenson, Esq., M.P. Second edition. Royal 16mo, price 3s. 6d. cloth; 4s. 6d., coloured, gilt edges.

" A most delicious volume of examples."--*Art Journal.*

Our Eastern Empire;

Or, Stories from the History of British India. Second Edition, with Continuation to the Proclamation of Queen Victoria. With Four Illustrations. Royal 16mo. cloth 3s. 6d.; 4s. 6d. coloured, gilt edges.

" These stories are charming, and convey a general view of the progress of our Empire in the East. The tales are told with admirable clearness."—*Athenæum.*

Might not Right;

Or, Stories of the Discovery and Conquest of America. Illustrated by J. Gilbert. Royal 16mo. 3s. 6d. cloth; 4s. 6d. coloured, gilt edges.

" With the fortunes of Columbus, Cortes, and Pizarro, for the staple of these stories, the writer has succeeded in producing a very interesting volume."—*Illustrated News.*

Tuppy;

Or the Autobiography of a Donkey. Illustrated by WEIR. Price 2s. 6d. cloth; 3s. 6d. coloured, gilt edges.

" A very intelligent donkey, worthy of the distinction conferred upon him by the artist." —*Art Journal.*

Rhymes and Pictures.

By WILLIAM NEWMAN. 12 Illustrations. Price 6d. plain, 1s. coloured. 2s. 6d. on linen, and bound in cloth.

1. The History of a Quartern Loaf.
2. The History of a Cup of Tea.
3. The History of a Scuttle of Coals.
4. The History of a Lump of Sugar.
5. The History of a Bale of Cotton.
6. The History of a Golden Sovereign.

*** Nos. 1 to 3 and 4 to 6, may be had bound in Two Volumes. Cloth price 2s. each, plain; 3s. 6d. coloured.

Hand Shadows,

To be thrown upon the Wall. By HENRY BURSILL. 1st & 2nd Series each containing Eighteen Original Designs. 4to. 2s. each plain; 2s. 6d. col.

" Uncommonly clever—some wonderful effects are produced."—*The Press.*

Old Nurse's Book of Rhymes, Jingles, and Ditties.

Illustrated by C. H. BENNETT. With Ninety Engravings. New Edition. Fcap. 4to., price 3s. 6d. cloth, plain, or 6s. coloured.

" The illustrations are all so replete with fun and imagination, that we scarcely know who will be most pleased with the book, the good-natured grandfather who gives it, or the chubby grandchild who gets it, for a Christmas-Box."—*Notes and Queries.*

Home Amusements.

A **Choice Collection** of Riddles, Charades, Conundrums, Parbur Games, and **Forfeits**. By PETER PUZZLEWELL, Esq., of Rebus Fall. New Edition, with Frontispiece by PHIZ. 16mo, 2s. 6d. cloth.

Clara Hope;

Or, the Blade and the Ear. By Miss MILNER. With Frontispiece by Birket Foster. Fcap. 8vo. price 3s. 6d. cloth; 4s. 6d. cloth elegant, gilt edges.

"A beautiful narrative, showing how **bad habits may be** eradicated, and evil tempers subdued."—*British Mother's Journal.*

BY W. H. G. KINGSTON.

Our Soldiers;

Or, Anecdotes of the Campaigns and Gallant Deeds of the British Army during the reign of Her Majesty Queen Victoria. By W. H. G. KINGSTON. With Frontispiece from a Painting in the Victoria Cross Gallery. Second Edition. Fcp. 8vo. price 3s. cloth; 3s. 6d. gilt edges.

Our Sailors;

Or, Anecdotes of the Engagements and **Gallant Deeds of** the British Navy during the reign of Her Majesty Queen Victoria. With Frontispiece. Second Edition. Price 3s. cloth; 3s. 6d. gilt edges.

"**These** volumes abundantly prove that both **our** officers and men in the Army and Navy, **have been** found **as** ready as ever to dare, and **to do as was** dared and done of yore."

W. H. G. KINGSTON'S BOOKS FOR BOYS.
With Illustrations. Fcap. 8vo. price 5s. each, cloth.

True Blue;

Or, the Life and Adventures of a British Seaman of the Old School.

"There is about all Mr. Kingston's tales a spirit of hopefulness, honesty, and cheery good principle, which makes them most wholesome, as well as most interesting reading."— *Era.*

"With the exception of Capt. Marryat, we know of no English author who will compare with Mr. Kingston as a writer of books of nautical adventure."—*Illustrated News.*

Will Weatherhelm;

Or, the Yarn of an Old Sailor about his Early Life and Adventures.

Fred Markham in Russia;

Or, the Boy Travellers in the Land of the Czar.

Salt Water;

Or Neil D'Arcy's Sea Life and Adventures.

Mark Seaworth;

A Tale of the Indian Ocean. Second Edition.

Peter the Whaler;

His early Life and Adventures in the Arctic Regions. Third Edition.

Distant Homes;

Or, the Graham Family in New Zealand. By Mrs. I. E. AYLMER.
With Illustrations. Price 3s. 6d. cloth; 4s. 6d. coloured, gilt edges.

"English children will be delighted with the history of the Graham Family, and be enabled to form pleasant and truthful conceptions of the 'Distant Homes' inhabited by their kindred."—*Athenæum*.

The Adventures and Experiences of Biddy Dork-

ING and of the FAT FROG. Edited by Mrs. S. C. HALL. Illustrated by H. Weir. 2s. 6d. cloth; 3s. 6d. coloured, gilt edges.

"Most amusingly and wittily told."—*Morning Herald*.

Historical Acting Charades;

Or, Amusements for Winter Evenings, by the author of "Cat and Dog," etc. New Edition. Fcap. 8vo., price 3s. 6d. cloth gilt edges.

"A rare book for Christmas parties, and of practical value."—*Illustrated News*.

The Story of Jack and the Giants:

With thirty-five Illustrations by RICHARD DOYLE. Beautifully printed.
New and Cheaper Edition. Fcap. 4to. price 2s. 6d. cloth; 3s. 6d.
coloured, extra cloth, gilt edges.

"In Doyle's drawings we have wonderful conceptions, which will secure the book a place amongst the treasures of collectors, as well as excite the imaginations of children."
—*Illustrated Times*.

Granny's Wonderful Chair;

And its Tales of Fairy Times. By FRANCES BROWNE. Illustrations by KENNY MEADOWS. 3s. 6d. cloth, 4s. 6d. coloured.

"One of the happiest blendings of marvel and moral we have ever seen."—*Literary Gazette*.

The Early Dawn;

Or, Stories to Think about. Illustrated by H. WEIR. Second Edition. Price 2s. 6d. cloth; 3s. 6d. coloured, gilt edges.

Angelo;

Or, the Pine Forest among the Alps. By GERALDINE E. JEWSBURY,
author of "The Adopted Child," etc. Illustrations by J. ABSOLON.
Second Edition. Price 2s. 6d. cloth; 3s. 6d. coloured, gilt edges.

"As pretty a child's story as one might look for on a winter's day."—*Examiner*.

Tales of Magic and Meaning.

Written and Illustrated by ALFRED CROWQUILL. 4to.; price 3s. 6d.
cloth; 4s. 6d. coloured.

"Cleverly written, abounding in frolic and pathos, and inculcates so pure a moral, that we must pronounce him a very fortunate little fellow, who catches these 'Tales of Magic,' as a windfall from 'The Christmas Tree'."—*Athenæum*.

Peter Parley's Fagots for the Fire Side;

Or, Tales of Fact and Fancy. Twelve Illustrations. New Edition. Fcap. 8vo.; 3s. 6d., cloth; 4s. 6d. coloured, gilt edges.

" A new book by Peter Parley is a pleasant greeting for all boys and girls, wherever the English language is spoken and read. He has a happy method of conveying information, while seeming to address himself to the imagination."—*The Critic.*

Letters from Sarawak,

Addressed to a Child; embracing an Account of the Manners, Customs, and Religion of the Inhabitants of Borneo, with Inciderts of Missionary Life among the Natives. By Mrs. M'DOUGALL. Fourth Thousand, with Illustrations. 3s. 6d. cloth.

" All is new, interesting, and admirably told."—*Church and State* **Gazette.**

Kate and Rosalind;

Or, Early Experiences. By the author of " Quicksands on Foreign Shores," etc. Fcap. 8vo, 3s. 6d. cloth; 4s. gilt edges.

" A book of unusual merit. The story is exceedingly well told, and the characters are drawn with a freedom and boldness seldom met with."—*Church of England Quarterly.*
" The Irish scenes are of an excellence that has not been surpassed since the best days of Miss Edgeworth."—*Fraser's Magazine.*

Clarissa Donnelly;

Or, The History of an Adopted Child. By GERALDINE E. JEWSBURY. With an Illustration by JOHN ABSOLON. Fcap. 8vo, 3s. 6d. cloth; 4s. gilt edges.

"With wonderful power, only to be matched by as admirable a simplicity, Miss Jewsbury has narrated the history of a child. For nobility of purpose, for simple, nervous writing, and for artistic construction, it is one of the most valuable works of the day."—*Lady's Companion.*

The Discontented Children;

And How they were Cured. By M. and E. KIRBY. Illustrated by H. K. BROWNE (Phiz.). Third edition, price 2s. 6d. cloth; 3s. 6d. coloured, gilt edges.

"We know no better method of banishing 'discontent' from school-room and nursery than by introducing this wise and clever story to their inmates."—*Art Journal.*

The Talking Bird;

Or, the Little Girl who knew what was going to happen. By M. and E. KIRBY. With Illustrations by H. K. BROWNE. Second Edition. Price 2s. 6d. cloth; 3s. 6d. coloured, gilt edges.

Julia Maitland;

Or, Pride goes before a Fall. By M. and E. KIRBY. Illustrated by ABSOLON. Price 2s. 6d. cloth; 3s. 6d. coloured, gilt edges.

" It is nearly such a story as Miss Edgeworth might have written on the same theme."— *The Press.*

COMICAL PICTURE BOOKS.

Each with Sixteen large Coloured Plates, price 2s. 6d., in fancy boards, or mounted on cloth, 1s. extra.

Picture Fables.

Written and Illustrated by ALFRED CROWQUILL.

The Careless Chicken;

By the BARON KRAKEMSIDES. By ALFRED CROWQUILL.

Funny Leaves for the Younger Branches.

By the BARON KRAKEMSIDES, of Burstenoudelafen Castle. Illustrated by ALFRED CROWQUILL.

Laugh and Grow Wise;

By the Senior Owl of Ivy Hall. With Sixteen large coloured Plates. Price 2s. 6d. fancy boards; or 3s. 6d. mounted on cloth.

The Remarkable History of the House that Jack

Built. Splendidly Illustrated and magnificently Illuminated by THE SON OF A GENIUS. Price 2s. in fancy cover.

"Magnificent in suggestion, and most comical in expression !"—*Athenæum.*

A Peep at the Pixies;

Or, Legends of the West. By Mrs. BRAY. Author of " Life of Stothard," "Trelawny," etc. With Illustrations by Phiz. Super-royal 16mo, price 3s. 6d. cloth; 4s. 6d. coloured, gilt edges.

" A peep at the actual Pixies of Devonshire, faithfully described by Mrs. Bray, is a treat. Her knowledge of the locality, her affection for her subject, her exquisite feeling for nature, and her real delight in fairy lore, have given a freshness to the little volume we did not expect. The notes at the end contain matter of interest for all who feel a desire to know the origin of such tales and legends."—*Art Journal.*

A BOOK FOR EVERY CHILD.

The Favourite Picture Book;

A Gallery of Delights, designed for the Amusement and Instruction of the Young. With several Hundred Illustrations from Drawings by J. ABSOLON, H. K. BROWNE (Phiz), J. GILBERT, T. LANDSEER, J. LEECH, J. S. PROUT, H. WEIR, etc. New Edition. Royal 4to., bound in a new and Elegant Cover, price 3s. 6d. plain; 7s. 6d. coloured; 10s. 6d. mounted on cloth and coloured.

Sunday Evenings with Sophia;

Or, Little Talks on Great Subjects. A Book for Girls. By LEONORA G. BELL. Frontispiece by J. ABSOLON. Fcap. 8vo, price 2s. 6d. cloth.

Blind Man's Holiday;

Or Short Tales for the Nursery. By the Author of "Mia and Charlie."
Illustrated by ABSOLON. 3s. 6d. cloth; 4s. 6d. coloured, gilt edges.

NEW AND BEAUTIFUL LIBRARY EDITION.

The Vicar of Wakefield;

A Tale. By OLIVER GOLDSMITH. Printed by Whittingham. With
Eight Illustrations by J. ABSOLON. Square fcap. 8vo, price 5s., cloth;
7s. half-bound morocco, Roxburghe style; 10s. 6d. antique morocco.

Mr. Absolon's graphic sketches add greatly to the interest of the volume: altogether,
it is as pretty an edition of the 'Vicar' as we have seen. Mrs. Primrose herself would
consider it 'well dressed.'"—*Art Journal.*

"A delightful edition of one of the most delightful of works: the fine old type and thick
paper make this volume attractive to any lover of books."—*Edinburgh Guardian.*

The Wonders of Home, in Eleven Stories.

By GRANDFATHER GREY. With Illustrations. Third and Cheaper
Edition. Royal 16mo., 2s. 6d. cloth; 3s. 6d. coloured, gilt edges.

"The idea is excellent, and its execution equally commendable. The subjects are well
selected, and are very happily told in a light yet sensible manner."—*Weekly News.*

Cat and Dog;

Or, Memoirs of Puss and the Captain. Illustrated by WEIR. Eighth
Edition. Super-royal 16mo, 2s. 6d. cloth; 3s. 6d. coloured, gilt edges.

"The author of this amusing little tale is, evidently, a keen observer of nature. The
illustrations are well executed; and the moral, which points the tale, is conveyed in the
most attractive form."—*Britannia.*

The Doll and Her Friends;

Or, Memoirs of the Lady Seraphina. By the Author of "Cat and
Dog." Third Edition. With Four Illustrations by H. K. BROWNE
(Phiz). 2s. 6d., cloth; 3s. 6d. coloured, gilt edges.

Tales from Catland;

Dedicated to the Young Kittens of England. By an OLD TABBY.
Illustrated by H. WEIR. Fourth Edition. Small 4to, 2s. 6d. plain;
3s. 6d. coloured, gilt edges.

"The combination of quiet humour and sound sense has made this one of the pleasantest
little books of the season."—*Lady's Newspaper.*

Scenes of Animal Life and Character.

From Nature and Recollection. In Twenty Plates. By J. B. 4to,
price 2s., plain; 2s. 6d., coloured, fancy boards.

"Truer, heartier, more playful, or more enjoyable sketches of animal life could
scarcely be found anywhere."—*Spectator.*

Anecdotes of the Habits and Instincts of Animals.

Third Edition. With Illustrations by HARRISON WEIR. Fcap. 8vo, 3s. 6d. cloth; 4s. gilt edges.

Anecdotes of the Habits and Instincts of Birds,

REPTILES, and FISHES. With Illustrations by HARRISON WEIR. Second Edition. Fcap. 8vo, 3s. 6d. cloth; 4s. gilt edges.

" Amusing, instructive, and ably written."—*Literary Gazette.*

" Mrs. Lee's authorities—to name only one, Professor Owen—are, for the most part first-rate.'—*Athenæum.*

Twelve Stories of the Sayings and Doings of

ANIMALS. With Illustrations by J. W. ARCHER. Third Edition. Super-royal 16mo, 2s. 6d. cloth; 3s. 6d. coloured, gilt edges.

Familiar Natural History.

With Forty-two Illustrations from Original Drawings by HARRISON WEIR. Super-royal 16mo, 3s. 6d. cloth; 5s. coloured gilt edges.

*** May be had in Two Volumes, 2s. each plain; 2s. 6d. Coloured, Entitled " British Animals and Birds." " Foreign Animals and Birds."

Playing at Settlers;

Or, the Fagot House. Illustrated by GILBERT. Second Edition. Price 2s. 6d. cloth; 3s. 6d. coloured, gilt edges.

Adventures in Australia;

Or, the Wanderings of Captain Spencer in the Bush and the Wilds. Second Edition. Illustrated by PROUT. Fcap. 8vo., 3s. 6d. cloth; 4s. gilt edges.

The African Wanderers;

Or, the Adventures of Carlos and Antonio; embracing interesting Descriptions of the Manners and Customs of the Western Tribes, and the Natural Productions of the Country. Fourth Edition. With Eight Engravings. Fcap. 8vo, 3s. 6d. cloth; 4s. gilt edges.

" For fascinating adventure, and rapid succession of incident, the volume is equal to any relation of travel we ever read."—*Britannia.*

Trees, Plants, and Flowers;

Their Beauties, Uses and Influences. By Mrs. R. LEE. With beautiful coloured Illustrations by J. ANDREWS. 8vo, price 10s. 6d., cloth elegant, gilt edges.

" The volume is at once useful as a botanical work, and exquisite as the ornament of a boudoir table."—*Britannia.* " As full of interest as of beauty."—*Art Journal.*

WORKS BY THE AUTHOR OF MAMMA'S BIBLE STORIES.

Fanny and her Mamma ;

Or, Easy Lessons for Children. In which it is attempted to bring Scriptural Principles into daily practice. Illustrated by J. GILBERT. Third Edition. 16mo, 2s. 6d. cloth; 3s. 6d. coloured, gilt edges.

"A little book in beautiful large clear type, to suit the capacity of infant readers, which we can with pleasure recommend."—*Christian Ladies' Magazine.*

Short and Simple Prayers,

For the Use of Young Children. With Hymns. Sixth Edition. Square 16mo, 1s. cloth.

" Well adapted to the capacities of children—beginning with the simplest forms which the youngest child may lisp at its mother's knee, and proceeding with those suited to its gradually advancing age. Special prayers, designed for particular circumstances and occasions, are added. We cordially recommend the book."—*Christian Guardian.*

Mamma's Bible Stories,

For her Little Boys and Girls, adapted to the capacities of very young Children. Twelfth Edition, with Twelve Engravings. 2s. 6d. cloth; 3s. 6d. coloured, gilt edges.

A Sequel to Mamma's Bible Stories.

Sixth Edition. Twelve Illustrations. 2s. 6d. cloth, 3s. 6d. coloured.

Scripture Histories for Little Children.

With Sixteen Illustrations, by JOHN GILBERT. Super-royal 16mo., price 2s. 6d. cloth; 3s. 6d. coloured, gilt edges.

CONTENTS.—The History of Joseph—History of Moses—History of our Saviour—The Miracles of Christ.

Sold separately: 6d. each, plain; 1s. coloured.

The Family Bible Newly Opened ;

With Uncle Goodwin's account of it. By JEFFERYS TAYLOR. Frontispiece by J. GILBERT. Fcap. 8vo, 3s. 6d. cloth.

" A very good account of the Sacred Writings, adapted to the tastes, feelings, and intelligence of young people."—*Educational Times.*

Good in Everything ;

Or, The Early History of Gilbert Harland. By MRS. BARWELL, Author of " Little Lessons for Little Learners," etc. Second Edition. Illustrations by GILBERT. 2s. 6d. cloth; 3s. 6d., coloured, gilt edges.

" The moral of this exquisite little tale will do more good than a thousand set tasks abounding with dry and uninteresting truisms."—*Bell's Messenger.*

THE FAVOURITE LIBRARY.

A Series of Works for the Young; each Volume with an Illustration by a well-known Artist. Price 1s. cloth.

1. THE ESKDALE HERD BOY. By LADY STODDART.
2. MRS. LEICESTER'S SCHOOL. By CHARLES and MARY LAMB.
3. THE HISTORY OF THE ROBINS. By MRS. TRIMMER.
4. MEMOIR OF BOB, THE SPOTTED TERRIER.
5. KEEPER'S TRAVELS IN SEARCH OF HIS MASTER.
6. THE SCOTTISH ORPHANS. By LADY STODDART.
7. NEVER WRONG; or, THE YOUNG DISPUTANT; and "IT WAS ONLY IN FUN."
8. THE LIFE AND PERAMBULATIONS OF A MOUSE.
9. EASY INTRODUCTION TO THE KNOWLEDGE OF NATURE. By MRS. TRIMMER.
10. RIGHT AND WRONG. By the Author of "ALWAYS HAPPY."
11. HARRY'S HOLIDAY. By JEFFERYS TAYLOR.
12. SHORT POEMS AND HYMNS FOR CHILDREN.

The above may be had Two **Volumes bound in One,** *at* **Two** *Shillings cloth.*

Glimpses of Nature;

And Objects of Interest described during a Visit to the Isle of Wight. Designed to assist and encourage Young Persons in forming habits of observation. By Mrs. LOUDON. Second Edition, enlarged. With Forty-one Illustrations. **3s. 6d. cloth.**

" We could not recommend a more valuable little volume. It is full of information, conveyed in the most agreeable manner."—*Literary Gazette.*

Tales of School Life.

By AGNES LOUDON. With Illustrations by JOHN ABSOLON. Second Edition. Royal 16mo, 2s. 6d. plain; 3s. 6d. coloured, gilt edges.

" These reminiscences of school days will be recognised as truthful pictures of every-day occurrence. The style is colloquial and pleasant, and therefore well suited to those for whose perusal it is intended."—*Athenæum.*

Kit Bam, the British Sinbad;

Or, the Yarns of an Old Mariner. By MARY COWDEN CLARKE, illustrated by GEORGE CRUIKSHANK. Fcap. 8vo, price 3s. 6d. cloth; 4s. gilt edges.

The Day of a Baby Boy;

A Story for a Young Child. By E. BERGER. With Illustrations by JOHN ABSOLON. Third Edition. Super-royal 16mo, price 2s. 6d. cloth; 3s. 6d. coloured, gilt edges.

" A sweet little book for the nursery."—*Christian Times.*

Visits to Beechwood Farm;

Or, Country Pleasures. By CATHERINE M. A. COUPER. Illustrations by ABSOLON. Small 4to, 3s. 6d., plain; 4s. 6d. coloured; gilt edges.

Stories of Julian and his Playfellows.

Written by HIS MAMMA. With Four Illustrations by JOHN ABSOLON. Second Edition. Small 4to., 2s. 6d., plain; 3s. 6d., coloured, gilt edges.

The Nine Lives of a Cat;

A Tale of Wonder. Written and Illustrated by C. H. BENNETT. Twenty-four Engravings. price 2s. cloth; 2s. 6d. coloured.

" Rich in the quaint humour and fancy that a man of genius knows how to spare for the enlivenment of children."—*Examiner.*

Maud Summers the Sightless:

A Narrative for the Young. Illustrated by ABSOLON. 3s. 6d. cloth; 4s. 6d. coloured, gilt edges.

London Cries and Public Edifices

Illustrated in Twenty-four Engravings by LUKE LIMNER; with descriptive Letter-press. Square 12mo, 2s. 6d. plain; 5s. coloured.

The Silver Swan;

A Fairy Tale. By MADAME DE CHATELAIN. Illustrated by JOHN LEECH. Small 4to, 2s. 6d. cloth; 3s. 6d. coloured, gilt edges.

Always Happy;

Or, Anecdotes of Felix and his Sister Serena. Nineteenth Edition, Illustrated by ANELAY. Royal 18mo, price 2s. cloth.

Anecdotes of Kings,

Selected from History; or, Gertrude's Stories for Children. With Engravings. 2s. 6d. plain; 3s. 6d. coloured.

Bible Illustrations;

Or, a Description of Manners and Customs peculiar to the East, and especially Explanatory of the Holy Scriptures. By the Rev. B. H. DRAPER. With Engravings. Fourth Edition. Revised by Dr. KITTO, Editor of " The Pictorial Bible," etc. 3s. 6d. cloth.

Trimmer's (Mrs.) Old Testament Lessons.
With 40 Engravings. 1s. 6d. cloth.

Trimmer's (Mrs.) New Testament Lessons.
With 40 Engravings. 1s 6d. cloth.

The Daisy,
With Thirty Wood Engravings. Price 1s. cloth. (1s. 6d. coloured.)

The Cowslip.
With Thirty Engravings. 1s. cloth. (1s. 6d. coloured.)

History of Prince Lee Boo.
Price 1s. cloth.

Dissections for Young Children;
In a neat box. Price 3s. 6d. each.

1. **Lives of** Joseph and Moses.
2. **History of Our Saviour.**
3. Mother Hubbard and Dog.
4. Life and Death of Cock Robin.

A Word to the Wise;
Or, Hints on the Current Improprieties of Expression in Writing and Speaking. By Parry Gwynne. 11th Thousand. 18mo. price 6d. sewed, or 1s. cloth. gilt edges.

"All who wish to mind their p's and q's should consult this little volume."—*Gentleman's Magazine.*

The British History briefly told,
and a Description of the Ancient Customs, Sports, and Pastimes of the English. Embellished with Portraits of the Sovereigns of England in their proper Costumes, and 18 other Engravings. 3s. 6d. cloth.

Chit-chat;
Or, Short Tales in Short Words. **By the author of** "Always Happy." **New** Edition. With **Eight Engravings. Price 2s.** 6d. cloth, 3s. 6d. coloured, gilt edges.

Conversations on the **Life of Jesus Christ.**
By a Mother. With 12 Engravings. 2s. 6d. plain; 3s. 6d. coloured.

Cosmorama.
The Manners, Customs, and Costumes of all Nations of the World described. By J. Aspin. With numerous Illustrations. 3s. 6d. plain; and 4s. 6d. coloured.

Easy Lessons;
Or, Leading-Strings to Knowledge. New Edition, with 8 Engravings. 2s. 6d. plain; 2s. 6d. coloured, gilt edges.

Key to Knowledge;
Or, Things in Common Use simply and shortly explained. By a MOTHER, Author of "Always Happy," etc. Thirteenth Edition. With Sixty Illustrations. 2s. 6d. cloth.

Facts to correct Fancies;
Or, Short Narratives compiled from the Biography o Remarkable Women. By a MOTHER. With Engravings, 3s. 6d. plain; 4s. 6d. coloured.

Fruits of Enterprise;
Exhibited in the Travels of Belzoni in Egypt and Nubia. Fourteenth Edition, with six Engravings by BIRKET FOSTER. Price 3s. cloth.

The Garden;
Or, Frederick's Monthly Instructions for the Management and Formation of a Flower Garden. Fourth Edition. With Engravings by SOWERBY. 3s. 6d. plain; or 6s. with the Flowers coloured.

How to be Happy;
Or, Fairy Gifts. to which is added a Selection of Moral Allegories. With Steel Engravings. Price 3s. 6d. cloth.

Infantine Knowledge.
A Spelling and Reading Book, on a Popular Plan. With numerous Engravings. Tenth Edition. 2s. 6d. plain; 3s. 6d. coloured, gilt edges.

The Ladder to Learning.
A Collection of Fables, arranged progressively in words of One, Two, and Three Syllables. Edited by Mrs. TRIMMER. With 79 Cuts. Nineteenth Edition. 2s. 6d. cloth.

Little Lessons for Little Learners.
In Words of One Syllable. By MRS. BARWELL. Tenth Edition, with numerous Illustrations. 2s. 6d. plain; 3s. 6d. coloured, gilt edges.

The Little Reader.
A Progressive Step to Knowledge. Fourth Edition with sixteen Plates. Price 2s. 6d. cloth.

Mamma's Lessons.
For her Little Boys and Girls. Fifteenth Edition, with eight Engravings. Price 2s. 6d. cloth; 3s. 6d. coloured, gilt edges.

The Mine;
Or, Subterranean Wonders. An Account of the Operations of the Miner and the Products of his Labours. By the late Rev. ISAAC TAYLOR. Sixth Edition, with numerous additions by Mrs. LOUDON. 45 Woodcuts and 16 Steel Engravings. 3s. 6d. cloth.

Rhoda;

Or, The Excellence of Charity. Fourth Edition. With Illustrations. 16mo, 2s. cloth.

The Students;

Or, Biographies of the Grecian Philosophers. 12mo, price 2s. 6d. cloth.

Stories of Edward and his little Friends.

With 12 Illustrations. Second Edition. 3s. 6d. plain; 4s. 6d. coloured.

Sunday Lessons for little Children.

By Mrs. BARWELL. Fourth Edition. 2s. 6d. plain; 3s. coloured.

EDUCATIONAL WORKS.

Rhymes of Royalty.

The History of England in Verse, from the Norman Conquest to the reign of QUEEN VICTORIA; with an Appendix, comprising a summary of the leading events in each reign. Fcap. 8vo, 2s. 6d. cloth.

True Stories from Ancient History,

Chronologically arranged from the Creation of the World to the Death of Charlemagne. Thirteenth Edition. With 24 Steel Engravings. 12mo, 5s. cloth.

True Stories from Modern History,

From the Death of Charlemagne to the present Time. Eighth Edition. With 24 Steel Engravings. 12mo, 5s. cloth.

The Modern British Plutarch;

Or, Lives of Men distinguished in the recent History of our Country for their Talents, Virtues and Achievements. By W. C. TAYLOR, LL.D. Author of "A Manual of Ancient and Modern History," etc. 12mo, Second Thousand. 4s. 6d. cloth; 5s. gilt edges.

"A work which will be welcomed in any circle of intelligent young persons."—*British Quarterly Review.*

Harry Hawkins's H-Book;

Shewing how he learned to aspirate his H's. Frontispiece by H. WEIR. Second Edition. Super-royal 16mo, price 6d.

" No family or school-room within, or indeed beyond, the sound of Bow bells, should be without this merry manual."—*Art Journal.*

Mrs. Trimmer's Concise History of England,

Revised and brought down to the present time by Mrs. MILNER. With Portraits of the Sovereigns in their proper costume, and Frontispiece by HARVEY. New Edition in One Volume. 5s. cloth.

Stories from the Old and New Testaments,
On an improved plan. By the Rev. B. H. DRAPER. With 48 Engravings. Fifth Edition. 12mo, 5s. cloth.

Pictorial Geography.
For the use of Children. Presenting at one view Illustrations of the various Geographical Terms, and thus imparting clear and definite ideas of their meaning. On a Large Sheet. Price 2s. 6d. in tints; 5s. on Rollers, varnished.

One Thousand Arithmetical Tests;
Or, The Examiner's Assistant. Specially adapted for Examination Purposes, but also suited for general use in Schools. By T. S. CAYZER, Head Master of Queen Elizabeth's Hospital, Bristol. Fourth Edition, revised and stereotyped. Price 1s. 6d. cloth.
₊ Answers to the above, 1s. 6d. cloth.

One Thousand Algebraical Tests;
On the same plan. Second Edition. 8vo., price 3s. 6d. cloth.
ANSWERS to the Algebraical Tests, price 2s. 6d. cloth.

Gaultier's Familiar Geography.
With a concise Treatise on the Artificial Sphere, and two coloured Maps, illustrative of the principal Geographical Terms. Sixteenth Edition. 16mo, 3s. cloth.

Butler's Outline Maps, and Key;
Or, Geographical and Biographical Exercises; with a Set of Coloured Outline Maps; designed for the Use of Young Persons. By the late WILLIAM BUTLER. Enlarged by the author's son, J. O. BUTLER. Thirty-fourth Edition, revised. 4s.

Every-Day Things;
Or, Useful Knowledge respecting the principal Animal, Vegetable, and Mineral Substances in common use. Second Edition. 18mo, 1s. 6d. cloth.
" A little encyclopædia of useful knowledge, deserving a place in every juvenile library."
—Evangelical Magazine.

Rowbotham's New and Easy Method of Learning
the FRENCH GENDERS. New Edition. 6d.

Bellenger's French Word and Phrase-book.
Containing a select Vocabulary and Dialogues, for the Use of Beginners. New Edition, 1s. sewed.

MARIN DE LA VOYE'S ELEMENTARY FRENCH WORKS.

Les Jeunes Narrateurs;

Ou Petits Contes Moraux. With a Key to the difficult words and phrases. Frontispiece. Second Edition. 18mo, 2s. cloth.
"Written in pure and easy French."—*Morning Post.*

The Pictorial French Grammar;

For the Use of Children. With Eighty Illustrations. Royal 16mo., price 1s. sewed; 1s. 6d. cloth.

Le Babillard.

An Amusing Introduction to the French Language. By a French Lady. Seventh Edition. With 16 Illustrations. 2s. cloth.

Der Schwätzer;

Or, the Prattler. An amusing Introduction to the German Language, on the Plan of "Le Babillard." 16 Illustrations. 16mo, price 2s. cloth.

Battle Fields.

A graphic Guide to the Places described in the History of England as the scenes of such Events; with the situation of the principal Naval Engagements fought on the Coast of the British Empire. By Mr. WAUTHIER, Geographer. On a large sheet 3s. 6d.; or on a roller, and varnished, 7s. 6d.

Tabular Views of the Geography and Sacred History

of PALESTINE, and of the TRAVELS of ST. PAUL. Intended for Pupil Teachers, and others engaged in Class Teaching. By A. T. WHITE. Oblong 8vo, price 1s., sewed.

The First Book of Geography;

Specially adapted as a Text Book for Beginners, and as a Guide to the Young Teacher. By HUGO REID, author of "Elements of Astronomy," etc. Fourth Edition, carefully revised. 18mo, 1s. sewed.
"One of the most sensible little books on the subject of Geography we have met with."
—*Educational Times.*

The Child's Grammar,

By the late LADY FENN, under the assumed name of Mrs. Lovechild. Fiftieth Edition. 18mo, 9d. cloth.

The Prince of Wales' Primer.

With 300 Illustrations by J. GILBERT. Price 6d., or 1s. Illuminated cover, gilt edges.

DURABLE NURSERY BOOKS,

MOUNTED ON CLOTH WITH COLOURED PLATES,

ONE SHILLING EACH.

1 Alphabet of Goody Two-Shoes.	8 Little Rhymes for Little Folks.
2 Cinderella.	9 Mother Hubbard.
3 Cock Robin.	10 Monkey's Frolic.
4 Courtship of Jenny Wren.	11 Old Woman and her Pig.
5 Dame Trot and her Cat.	12 Puss in Boots.
6 History of an Apple Pie.	13 Tommy Trip's Museum of
7 House that Jack built.	Birds.

BY THOMAS DARNELL.

PARSING SIMPLIFIED: An Introduction and Companion to all Grammars; consisting of Short and Easy Rules (with Parsing Lessons to each) whereby young Students may, in a short time, be gradually led through a knowledge of the several Elementary Parts of Speech to a thorough comprehension of the grammatical construction of the most complex sentences of our ordinary Authors, either in Prose or Poetry, by THOMAS DARNELL. Price 1s. cloth.

" Sound in principle, singularly felicitous in example and illustration, and though brief, thoroughly exhaustive of the subject. The boy who will not learn to parse on Mr. Darnell's plan is not likely to do so on any other.—*Morning Post.*

GEORGE DARNELL'S EDUCATIONAL WORKS.

The attention of all interested in the subject of Education is invited to these Works, now in extensive use throughout the Kingdom, prepared by Mr. George Darnell, a Schoolmaster of many years' experience.

1. COPY BOOKS.—A SHORT AND CERTAIN ROAD TO A GOOD HANDWRITING, gradually advancing from the Simple Stroke to a superior Small-hand.

LARGE POST, Sixteen Numbers, 6d. each.

FOOLSCAP, Twenty Numbers, to which are added Three Supplementary Numbers of Angular Writing for Ladies, and One of Ornamental Hands. Price 3d. each.

⁎ This series may also be had on very superior paper, marble covers, 4d. each.

"For teaching writing I would recommend the use of Darnell's Copy Books. I have noticed a marked improvement wherever they have been used."—*Report of Mr. Maye* (*National Society's Organizer of Schools*) *to the Worcester Diocesan Board of Education.*

2. GRAMMAR, made intelligible to Children, price 1s. cloth.

3. ARITHMETIC, made intelligible to Children, price 1s. 6d. cloth.

⁎ Key to Parts 2 and 3, price 1s. cloth.

4. READING, a Short and Certain Road to, price 6d. cloth.

WERTHEIMER, LEA AND CO., CIRCUS PLACE, FINSBURY CIRCUS.